THE INTERIOR LITURGY
OF THE
OUR FATHER

THE INTERIOR LITURGY OF THE OUR FATHER

R. THOMAS RICHARD

Fidelis Publications
P.O. Box 335
Beaufort, SC 29902

ISBN 0-9759466-0-9

© Copyright 2004 by R. Thomas Richard
All rights reserved

Library of Congress catalogue number 2004091481

Printing Information:

Current Printing - first digit - 1   2   3   4   5   6   7   8   9   10

Year of Current Printing - first year shown:

2004   2005   2006   2007   2008   2009   2010   2011   2012   2013

Dedication

It is an awesome gesture, to offer some poor work to God! Yet why else labor, except to hope that in some small way the work is good, in His sight? May this book be a help to those who seek Him! May the glimpse that He gave me, into this most beautiful prayer the *Our Father*, serve to help others as well who long to find blessed communion in Him.

Many have helped me in the process of bringing this book to completion. One who has been with me as loving companion and friend from its inception, however, must be noted. My most treasured gift from God, my wife Deborah has helped me unfailingly and always to seek Him and listen to Him. Gratefully, with her, I dedicate this book to God to use as He will. We pray that it might be used toward the renewal of His holy Church.

Contents

THE INTERIOR LITURGY
OF THE
OUR FATHER

The Interior Liturgy of the *Our Father*

Prologue

The Need for Prayer

The world needs to find God! Every human person was created by God and for God; no person can ever find himself - his happiness, fulfillment and peace - without God. We find evidence of God everywhere, and anywhere, because God has created all that is. Yet God Himself, so to speak, is found finally only within, only in an interior awareness enlightened by His grace. This awareness, this gift, is a facet of that personal communion with God that is called prayer. We find God in prayer.

It would be simplistic to say that we find God only in prayer. We find God also through the help of other persons, because of His intention. Yet again by His intention, we find God most easily and beautifully through people of prayer. Persons of prayer have a kind of transparency, and through them we can sense God. Persons of prayer have an anointing - an unction - giving the glow of His presence. God is a luminance in them. Persons of prayer have a habitual warmth and attractiveness, yet at the same time they hold a fearful mystery. God is fearsome; all the while He calls us.

Because the Church is given the ministry of calling others in His name, the Church continues to be in great need, to remain in prayer and to grow in prayer. The Church is called to holiness, both because He who loves her is holy, and also because the work He has given her to do demands her sanctity. He has set her apart, to gather all into His oneness. We come to know Him in prayer; we begin to love Him in prayer. We serve Him rightly, only through union with Him in prayer. We must remain in Him: this remaining is the life of prayer.

Unless our witness of Him is to remain external only, we

need to grow in prayer. Unless our Christian life is to be only nominal, only ceremonial, only by rote obedience and without vitality, we need to grow in prayer. We can thank God that by the nature of love, love wants to grow! We can be grateful that love cannot be satisfied with mere formality, or superficial relationship. We have heard Him call; we have known His embrace. How now can we be satisfied with anything less, than to remain in Him, in a life of prayer?

This book

   This book is offered as a help for Christians who earnestly want to grow in Christ. The book is concerned primarily with prayer - specifically the prayer given us by Jesus, the *Our Father* - yet through prayer, the entire spiritual journey is considered. This book presents the *Our Father* as not only the foundation for our life of prayer, for it is much more. The *Our Father* is also our personal guide to the interior liturgy: to the saving work of Christ in us, as we journey with him in discipleship. His work in us - His saving liturgy within us - has a plan, a pattern and a form: His liturgy is described by the prayer He gave us, the *Our Father*.

   This book is intended not to be merely talk about prayer, but a personal and helpful guide to the spiritual life: the life of prayer. I hope that this book will help the reader listen to Jesus and to His Church, hearing the trustworthy direction He gives us in His Church for our interior journey. This book cannot be a substitute for a good spiritual director, but it could be a good supplement to one. It will, I hope, also be helpful to those who have not been able to find a good spiritual director - and there are many such searchers. It can be a difficult task to find good, faithful, substantial and helpful personal guidance in spiritual matters! This book is offered in response to the need.

   This book is of two parts. Part I is the introduction to the prayer, but please do not pass over this introduction to get more quickly to Part II, the prayer itself! This introduction, in four chapters, can help the reader approach the too-familiar prayer afresh and perhaps from a new perspective. In this way the multifaceted and multidimensional aspects of the prayer, presented in Part II, can be more easily recognized and perhaps more deeply appreciated.

It is true that the perspective presented here is somewhat unusual, discovering within the *Our Father* the entire spiritual journey, summarized. Yet it is also true that the journey so discovered is not at all innovative, but is merely the traditional path seen so commonly in our graced tradition, in our saints and fathers and doctors. The pattern of our spiritual journey in Christ is unfolded here in the *Our Father*, but we will see the same pattern described consistently in traditional Catholic spirituality: the three ways or stages of the interior life, and the seven mansions in St. Teresa's *Interior Castle*.

To grow in Christ means to grow in the four dimensions or "pillars" of the Christian life: His revealed truth in the doctrines of the faith, His grace in the sacraments, His life lived in Christian morality, and communion with Him in Christian prayer. This book approaches His life through the dimension of prayer, yet not for a moment can prayer, and the interior life, be separated from the wholeness and unity of His life. The interior life is fully and authentically life, and it proves itself in the completeness of His life in human expression. The interior life naturally and supernaturally bears the fruit becoming of it: a growing light of understanding of God as revealed to His Church, a growing embrace of the sacramental grace of Christ, a growing moral fidelity to His life lived, and a growing personal communion with Him in the dialogue of prayer.

I hope that this work will be helpful to many, from diverse backgrounds and formation. An understanding of the traditional three stages of the interior life would be helpful, and for this reason my first book, *The Ordinary Path to Holiness*[1], would be a good introduction to the basic spirituality from which this work springs. The direct relationship of the seven stations of the interior liturgy, to the seven mansions in St. Teresa's *Interior Castle*, is also presented in that book.

This book is in a sense a sequel to *The Ordinary Path to Holiness*. That book attempted to present an introduction to traditional Catholic understanding of the spiritual life. It was written in the challenging, sometimes troubling and yet opportune situation of our time. In our time, many Catholic adults lack a solid adult catechesis in the Faith, and lack also guidance in the interior life. Many Catholics are sadly confused in their faith because of intrusions of secular thought and of New Age spiritualities. The Ordinary Path was written to help the ordinary Catholic understand our beautiful heritage of authentically Christian spirituality. This present work, The Interior Liturgy, follows that first work as a specific guide and companion along the pilgrimage: to help the Catholic enter and grow personally in that authentic life of prayer.

I have attempted to use few references in the book, and to depend mostly upon two crucial sources for Catholics, the Bible and the *Catechism*. The life of prayer of course is not a merely intellectual pursuit. I hope that this work is not seen as a study, but rather received as a guide and companion for Christians personally and actively striving to grow in prayer. A "companion" is literally one who shares bread with another. I hope that I, with this book, may be a companion with you, the reader. We are fellow pilgrims on the same journey, with similar struggles and hopes, hungers and fears. May the Lord give us the grace we need, as we seek His nourishing bread together in faith and with confident hope, that we might live the holy charity of Christ in our lives.

PART I - INTRODUCTION TO THE PRAYER

Chapter 1. The Meaning of Liturgy

Liturgy

The words of the *Our Father* have power, flowing from their source, God the Holy Trinity. Jesus the Son taught us this prayer. This prayer, if we open ourselves in sincerity and understanding in our praying, will cause a great work to proceed in the depths of our souls. The work, quiet yet transforming, is an intimate and personal participation in the divine act that stands at the center of all human history – the great and saving work of Jesus Christ.

The interior and personal work of Christ in the soul, articulated through the prayer the *Our Father*, is a liturgy – it is a divine work and a human work within the great Paschal Mystery of Christ. It is interior – internal – within the souls of persons. It is a work for salvation that is guided according to the prayer, the *Our Father*.

God will work a beautiful work – a liturgy – within us, if we will allow Him, and welcome Him. In this book we will look upon the *Our Father* and enter its prayer in the light of holy liturgy, and we will see this holy liturgy in the light of the universal and yet profoundly personal saving work of Jesus Christ. That is, as I pray the *Our Father*, He works and guides and unfolds His saving work in me.

For many Catholics liturgy is simply the Mass, celebrated in the sanctuary of the church. Liturgy commonly refers to the celebration, the ceremony of the worship of the Church in Holy Mass. More generally, Catholics refer in the word liturgy to the celebration of every sacrament: there is a liturgy of Baptism, a liturgy of Reconciliation, a liturgy of Ordination, a liturgy of Holy Eucharist, and so on.

Liturgy originally and in its secular uses, from the Greek leitourgia, meant a public service - some work of or on behalf of the people. Liturgy today in the Church has its deepest meaning tied intimately to work. The word liturgy was taken into the language of the Church to mean the magnificent work of Christ for our salvation and life. Liturgy for us, then, is His divine work accomplished in His sacred humanity - yet it is also our work, in Christ.

The interior work: the liturgy within

Restoring life - uncovering the crucial meaning of each human person - is the work of Christ the Son; it is His ministry. Restoring life - unveiling the treasure given - is therefore also the mission of His Church: it is her apostolate and her participation in the saving work of God. Restoring life - revealing in works and words His Good News - is then the liturgy of the Church. In the unfolding celebration of her liturgy, especially in the Holy Mass, the Church is working the works of God, bringing again His life to the world.

There is another liturgy unfolding, celebrated: an interior and personal liturgy in concert with the holy work of the Church. This other liturgy is also bringing forth its growth - first the leaf, then the head, then the full grain in the head. (Mk 4:26-29) This other liturgy is working toward the harvest season in an interior way, celebrating and participating with the Church yet within, immediate and personal. Each person is called to return to God: God loves each person; God calls each person. The return to God, to communion in His life, is our fully personal and human vocation, experienced in the human realities of time moving through moments and acts experienced in words and works.

Salvation is not accomplished in an instant! It is accomplished as a work, in a human life, through a process in time. The work of the salvation of a human person is accomplished and prayed in the interior liturgy of the person. This interior liturgy is a work and a prayer parallel to the liturgy of the Church, sharing in its actions and meaning. The interior liturgy has actions of change, of formation and of transformation in the soul, stage by stage progressing toward the final purpose of human life.

These two liturgies move and develop together: the liturgy of the Church, celebrated especially at Holy Mass, and the liturgy celebrated in the soul of each person. Each liturgy is the outworking of life, the unfolding of grace, the story and the realization of God's saving work. To understand one is to understand the other; to grow in one is to grow in the other, to celebrate one is to celebrate the other. We are surrounded by symbols! Seeing the inward in the things outside, realizing that my personal and inner pilgrimage is not hidden but is our common struggle, our shared privilege: realizing in Holy Mass the fulfillment of all human life – this is a beautiful gift, a communion and a reunion. In God we find God; we find ourselves; we find one another.

The sanctuary of meeting

In the interior of the soul is a sanctuary, a meeting place reserved for God. How we long for that meeting! Our whole life long, every moment is in some way an anticipation – or a substitution – for that moment! The entire journey of our life is in some way a search for – or a fleeing from – that place of meeting. God made us, and we are made for Him: not to be used by Him like some thing, but to return as free persons to His love.

In the history of man, the meeting place with God was at first immediate and intimate: in the Garden, before his fall, man walked with God in friendship. The liturgy of man, his work of worship, filled his day and embraced his night. In the beginning, the interior life of man was expressed in integrity and simplicity in the work he was given to do: to care for the Garden, and to be fruitful in love.

Following his fall into sin, however, man became lost, awaking as a foreigner in a foreign land. Familiar yet different, sensed yet not known: both land and God became estranged, and his meeting place was gone.

Yet we were made for friendship, to be at home with the One who made us. In the proper time, God began His restoration. Through Abraham, God reestablished a family under His name. Through Moses, God gave them a tent of meeting: a meeting place they could carry with them, in their exodus and journey to a new land of old promise. Through the son of David, Solomon, a temple for worship was built: of the design given by God, of the work of human hands, a meeting place for God and man stood on holy ground. God is so patient, so careful of our freedom! God did not violate the confused conscience of His creatures: He would not enter, before we could invite Him in. Yet it is within each person that the meeting place must be!

In Jesus Christ God came to man finally, fully, completely. Who could have imagined that the meeting place would come in this way? God met man so humbly, through the simple handmaid Mary, not before her "Yes" welcomed Him and received Him into her life. God met man so intimately within Mary that the meeting of natures, both human and divine, embraced in a single Person Jesus Christ. In Jesus, the meeting place of God and man was forever made clear. God will meet with human persons in His way: a way most mysterious and complete.

Only after the out-pouring at Pentecost was the mysterious way of God made clear. God would meet us within us: the sanctuary of meeting ultimately and finally is within. More interior than the marrow of our bones, more immediate than the blood within our hearts is the place reserved for God. The longing, the profound and deep thirst for God so within us that it is obscure even to us, draws us to the place awaiting: the sanctuary, the meeting place within.

Work

To understand and appreciate the meaning of liturgy in its true beauty, we must understand and appreciate the meaning of work in its beauty and dignity. Liturgy is inseparable from work because liturgy is a work. And where does religion - where does worship - enter? Worship is the religious dimension that elevates the activity of secular human work to become liturgy, and worship is worship because of love[2]. Our work in Christ is liturgy, in other words, and not merely "work" as we commonly think of work, because of the transforming and ennobling power of divine love. Work, in its full intended meaning, is love expressed. Liturgy is divine love unveiled in the created world of matter and space and time.

There are at least two negative connotations bound with work, which need to be clarified here. In the sad divisions of Christianity, among some of our separated Protestant brethren, there is a strongly negative connotation associated with religious works. In Scripture we are exhorted to turn away from the "dead works" of religious hypocrisy (i.e. Heb 6:1, 9:14) in order to serve the true and living God through faith. The gospels present us with many scenes of conflict; the religious men of Judea were scandalized and angered by Jesus, and Jesus called these religious men hypocrites. Jesus condemned their religious works as done not in faith but for human praise: "They do all their deeds to be seen by men." (Mt

23:5) Indeed, Paul wrote, "For we hold that a man is justified by faith apart from works of law." (Rom 3:28)

Some Protestants then find in Scripture a basis to become very suspicious of any works done for God, and they separate salvation from any human works:

> For by grace you have been saved through faith; and this is not your own doing, it is the gift of God - not because of works, lest any man should boast.[3]

Some Protestant Christians then believe that we are saved by faith alone, completely apart from works. This thinking leads, unfortunately, to a wrong sense of faith, of works, of grace, and of salvation itself. It leads some, also and unfortunately, to their misunderstanding and their condemnation of the Catholic liturgy. These misinterpret the liturgy as only "dead works" of religious pretense and hypocrisy. They misinterpret the beautiful gestures of the liturgy - the incense, the kneeling, the prayer responses, the vestments and the movements - as so much human emptiness. These misjudgments of theirs are grievous and even tragic, adding as they do to the continuing divisions of Christianity.

It is important to know that such misunderstandings exist, so that we might respond to them more completely when the chance arises. It is good to know that the very next verse in Scripture, following the one quoted above, assures us: "For we are his workmanship, created in Christ Jesus for good works, which God prepared beforehand, that we should walk in them." (Eph 2:10) We are created specifically for good works! The letter of James states strongly, "faith apart from works is dead." (James 2:26) The good works that bring us to joy in Christ include all the works of authentic faith and genuine love, and are celebrated most completely in the liturgy of the Church.

The second negative connotation of work, to which we

should give note, is that sense that work is itself a burden, indeed part of the curse and penalty of sin. God said to Adam after his sin, "In the sweat of your face you shall eat bread till you return to the ground, for out of it you were taken; you are dust, and to dust you shall return" (Gen 3:19) This well describes the work that most of us experience! For so many, work is the joyless price we pay for the money we need to live. For many, work is endured, not enjoyed.

Work is, however, not the penalty for sin: it is essential to our human nature. God made man in His image, and gave him the vocation of work in the created world:

> So God created man in his own image, in the image of God he created him; male and female he created them. And God blessed them, and God said to them, "Be fruitful and multiply, and fill the earth and subdue it; and have dominion ... over every living thing that moves upon the earth."[4]

The *Catechism* clarifies this: "Human work proceeds directly from persons created in the image of God and called to prolong the work of creation by subduing the earth, both with and for one another."[5]

Our work is to be our expression of the divine image. God gave mankind a sanctuary, the Garden of Eden, in which to express in his human ways this glory of his being: "The LORD God took the man and put him in the garden of Eden to till it and keep it." (Gen 2:15) This vocation was not lost to man by his sin, but he indeed lost his way even to himself. In Christ, our vocation is restored. In Christ, the work intended to humanity becomes again our possibility, our vocation, our joy. In Christ who said, "My Father is working still, and I am working," we also find the meaning of our work. (Jn 5:17)

Work should be seen, then, not as mere human hypocrisy, as "dead works" that insult the gift of faith. Indeed, good works prove the life of our faith! Neither should work be thought of as drudgery inflicted upon us by God as a punishment for sin - indeed, work began when God accomplished the work of creation, and then rested on the seventh day "from all his work which he had done…." (Gen 2:3) Christ Jesus was not ashamed to identify His actions and purpose with that of the Father who sent Him: His Father was working still, and so He worked. Work for a Christian is to be part of his life of worship, a collaboration in Christ with God and with one another toward the restoration of the world to God's beautiful intention.

It is good also to ponder the place that work - or activity in general - is to have because of the nature of the human person. The human person is a unity of body and soul, having a material part and a spiritual part yet brought together into one nature, human nature. The awesome dignity of the human person, made as he is in the divine image, holds also this mystery of his unity of body and soul. The human person is one person, yet he is both matter and spirit and his peace requires a certain unity of those two very different realities.

My integrity as a person requires the unity of my body with my soul. I cannot live in peace and happiness if the acts of my body conflict with the desires of my soul! If my mind and heart give assent to the truth of Christ, I cannot happily continue to live in sin and disobedience! The human heart recoils against the lie of hypocrisy: we know within ourselves that our lives must be consistent with the truths that we hold. In this way the simple meaning of the Catholic faith is clear, that "faith without works is dead." The faith we hold within our hearts must find expression in our bodies, our lives. We must live in integrity, otherwise we betray ourselves as well as our God.

Good works are as normal to the human person restored in Christ as good fruit is to the healthy vine. We are made to express through our bodies, in our material being, the spiritual truth entrusted to us interiorly in the soul. The interior life cannot be separated from the exterior and public human life, except at the peril of profound disturbance and disquiet. We are made to be one person, with our "yes" as "yes", and our "no" as "no". The good work - hence the liturgy - of a human person is to be as beautiful and as natural as the fruitful vine.

Liturgy: the work of Christ

The work of Christ is the light that illuminates all our human works, and His work is celebrated in the liturgy. It is difficult to overstate the place of the liturgy in the faith of the Church! "The liturgy is the summit toward which the activity of the Church is directed; it is also the font from which all her power flows."[6] The liturgy is our part in the great saving work of Christ - our ministry in Him is our ultimate vocation, hence it is the summit of our activity; and this ministry is possible only in Him and through Him, hence it is the font of our power. The *Catechism* asserts for us in brevity a truth that probes the grandeur of the divine mystery of God Himself; in His great love for mankind in Christ, He invites us into His work.

> All the liturgies of the Church point toward the celebration of the Holy Eucharist. The Eucharist is "the source and summit of the Christian life."[7] "The other sacraments, and indeed all ecclesiastical ministries and works of the apostolate, are bound up with the Eucharist and are oriented toward it. For in the blessed Eucharist is contained the whole spiritual good of the Church, namely Christ himself, our Pasch."[8]

The liturgies of the Church recall the saving work of Christ; they also re-present them; they also enact them, inserting the saving work of Christ into our time and place. The celebrated liturgies of the Church are the saving work of Christ continued in the world and made present to mankind.

Liturgy in the Church today, as in the beginning, has a

prescribed form and sequence - a structure - that enables our participation. The Church in Vatican II calls for our participation as individual persons to be "full, conscious and active"[9] . We need to be fully engaged in the communal worship of the Church as persons. The beautiful prayers, gestures, actions, responses and songs of the gathered community are offered by persons, who must contribute their full presence as persons.

Liturgy and faith are most intimately linked.

The Church's faith precedes the faith of the believer who is invited to adhere to it. When the Church celebrates the sacraments, she confesses the faith received from the apostles - whence the ancient saying: lex orandi, lex credendi .... The law of prayer is the law of faith: the Church believes as she prays. Liturgy is a constitutive element of the holy and living Tradition.[10]

This book is concerned with that interior and personal work of salvation within the soul of the person: the interior liturgy. This interior liturgy also has form and sequence, also including gestures, actions, responses and songs within, which then find exterior human expression in the moral and human life of the person. There is an interior work in process in every human person! There is an interior developing life either toward God, or away from Him - either toward our intended destiny, or in escape from it. The interior liturgy is that work of Christ in the soul, with our personal response and participation, that is ordered toward Him.

The interior liturgy then is a communion of life and prayer, prayer and life. Its source is Christ - His saving work, His gift, His love. The interior liturgy is wed to the communal liturgy of the Church, each exchanging life with the other. The interior liturgy of the person, as also the communal liturgy of the Church, is inseparable from prayer: liturgy is prayer, in the fullest senses of both words.

The liturgy is also a participation in Christ's own prayer addressed to the Father in the Holy Spirit. In the liturgy, all Christian prayer finds its source and goal. Through the liturgy the inner man is rooted and grounded in "the great love with which [the Father] loved us" in his beloved Son. It is the same "marvelous work of God" that is lived and internalized by all prayer, "at all times in the Spirit."[11]

In this book the interior liturgy, and hence our personal life of communion with God, is shown to be enlightened, guided, described, formed and informed by the prayer given us by Jesus, the *Our Father*. This simple yet comprehensive prayer answers the request of disciples, "Lord, teach us to pray," more fully and completely than we probably imagine! We will consider the life of prayer through this particular prayer. We will find treasures and wisdom that drive us to our knees before God in thanksgiving; He gives far beyond what we know to ask.

<u>The liturgy of trinitarian love</u>

The liturgy of the Son is a work of love. God so loved the world - every human person who ever lived or would live - that He sent His only Son. The work of salvation is then the work of love of the Father, in sending the Son. It is a liturgy of love of the Son, in His incarnation, His passion, His death and resurrection. It is His work of love continued, in sending the Holy Spirit to the Church, enabling her to be His Body and His Spouse and the living temple of God among men. It is a liturgy of love of God the Holy Trinity, because God is love and all His works are love. It is a supreme and most personal work of love, worked within every man and woman: this interior liturgy is the work of recalling every man and woman to our original vocation. The intention of God in our creation is that beatitude of communion in the love of God the Holy Trinity.

The interior liturgy is a work in which the love of God

develops in the soul of a human person. The interior liturgy is therefore the work of our salvation, because our salvation rests upon our love:

> And behold, a lawyer stood up to put him to the test, saying, "Teacher, what shall I do to inherit eternal life?" He said to him, "What is written in the law? How do you read?"
>
> And he answered, "You shall love the Lord your God with all your heart, and with all your soul, and with all your strength, and with all your mind; and your neighbor as yourself."
>
> And he said to him, "You have answered right; do this, and you will live."[12]

By the grace of God, through our faith in Christ, this saving love is received into the human soul and begins to grow. This saving love is at first only the sense that somehow God loves me! What great joy in our hearts, in knowing this! This is only the beginning, however, and the divine reality of love is intended to grow, and develop, and bear beautiful fruit for our even greater joy, and for the glory of God.

The love of God, or more precisely, divine charity, develops and grows in the interior liturgy. "The love of God" is a simple phrase, that contains deep and profound meaning. This means both our "love for God", as well as our sharing in "love that comes from God and is of Him." The word charity means all this: charity is love for God because of who He is as God, and love for others because of God. The love of God, then, or charity, is an infinitely deep mystery from within God Himself. The love of God is so intimate to God, so bound to His divine nature, that we are told that God is love. (1 Jn 4:8, 16)

The love of God is our vocation, our destiny. God wants us - us poor human creatures - to share with Him in some way, the infinite joy of infinite divine love. For that reason, because of God's will for our sharing in love, He has commanded this to us as the overriding imperative of human life. We must love, if we are to live. We must love God wholly, in the fullness and integrity of ourselves, and we must love others in this same love. This imperative is inscribed upon our hearts and souls: to be ourselves, to be who we are, we must love. We are made in the divine image; we must love.

Christ came to give us love. He came not only to love us, but to shepherd us into the life of God who is love. In the beginning, we know only that he has loved us, and that He loves us. This is wonderful news! Yet there is more to love than only being loved: we are called, in a sense and by participation, to be love with Him and in Him who is love.

The saving work of Christ in us, then, is a work of the development of love[13]. In the beginning we come to believe that God loves us, and we love God in return because of the great good that He does for us. This is a beginning, but it is self-centered. We love God but only for what He does or can do for us: this is only the faint beginning of charity. This is the first movement of God in the soul, yet only the first. This is the first movement, then, of the interior liturgy.

In the second movement of the interior liturgy, there is revealed to the person, interiorly, something of the transcendent glory of God. In traditional Catholic spirituality this is called the illuminative stage, or the stage of the proficients. In this movement, the soul is awakened to the splendor and glory of God as He is in Himself! The beauty, the majesty, the perfection of God is seen in some limited way in the soul, and in response the person begins to love God not merely for what God can do for him, but because of who God is. This is a major development toward true charity. It is not complete, because there remains in the soul still, traces of self-centeredness. Love is greatly developed in this person, yet not completely or perfectly. There remains still "mercenary" love, still concerns with self above God.

In the third and final movement of the interior liturgy, the love of God is brought to maturity and true fruitfulness. In this movement, the soul is brought to love God above all and to love others only in God. In traditional Catholic spirituality this is called the unitive stage, or the stage of the perfect. This is the full meaning of charity, made real in a human person. Here the fundamental commandment to love is lived in the obedience of faith.

We are called to love God in the community of faith, saying to Him, "Our Father who art in heaven." To love God for who God is, in the fullness of charity, we embrace the mystery of the name of God - Father, Son and Holy Spirit - and we pray, "hallowed be thy name." To love God in the community of faith among persons we pray for the perfection and fruitfulness of the Church: "thy kingdom come." To love God unto the perfection and fruitfulness of the Church, we pray for the obedience of faith in her: "thy will be done on earth as it is in heaven." To love God in His Church, we pray for the heavenly food to nurture us: "give us this day our daily bread." To love God in receiving His divine food, we must confess our sin, and enter His mercy: "forgive us our trespasses, as we forgive those who trespass against us." To love God in repentance and conversion, we must turn to Him in our struggle against the love of sin within us: "lead us not into temptation." To love God in repentance and conversion, we must repent, convert and believe the good news: "deliver us from evil."

The interior liturgy is a work of love. It is the love of Christ enabling love in us: a love that grows and develops, maturing into a more and more authentic share in the holy love of God. In Christ, this love descends. It is out-poured from the inner life of God the Holy Trinity, down to us who though we were lost, we were made in the divine image and intended for divine communion. The liturgy in us, however, is an ascent. We experience love growing in us, upward as it were, from the tiny seed given us in faith and Baptism, intended to mature to sanctity and fruitfulness.

The mystery of the petitions of the *Our Father* will be discussed in more detail later, and will be presented also as we consider the petitions one at a time. For now, we note that the prayer as we were given it and as we pray it, is a prayer that begins with our highest desire in the fullness of love, and descends down to our first plea in the darkness of sin: "Lord, save me from this evil!" Our response - the journey of our Christian life and the unfolding of His work in us - is a liturgy that is celebrated in stations that begin at the close of the prayer, in our struggle against evil, and that then proceed station by station in ascent toward communion in the holy name.

Liturgy and Life

The communal liturgy and the interior liturgy

There is an intrinsic essential unity among what we perceive as different expressions of the great saving work of Christ. We see different facets; in truth there is one precious reality. We see different dimensions and moments: in truth there is one economy of salvation, one work of redemption. This great work is ordered to one end: "The ultimate end of the whole divine economy is the entry of God's creatures into the perfect unity of the Blessed Trinity."[14]

It is important for every Catholic to keep in mind the inseparable unity of God's works for salvation: the communal liturgy and the interior liturgy. It is important to remember, as we grow in prayer and in our whole life in Christ, that the liturgy of the Church is vitally bound together with the interior liturgy. In the beginning this unity and interdependence may not be obvious! Yet this coherence of the liturgies - the interior and personal with the communal and ecclesial - cannot be divided without serious injury to the person in his spirit and indeed in his humanity.

The communal liturgy nourishes, forms and guides the interior liturgy. The interior liturgy resonates with, responds to, and is the personal witness and confirmation of the communal liturgy. The interior liturgy rejoices in affirmation, the "yes" of the human person, in the testimony of the Holy Spirit that is spoken in the communal liturgy. The communal liturgy illuminates that interior work, as a mother guides her child.

Christ is really present in many ways in the Church: "in his word, in his Church's prayer, 'where two or three are gathered in my name,' (Mt 18:20) in the poor, the sick, and the imprisoned (Cf. Mt 25:31-46), in the sacraments of which he is the author, in the sacrifice of the Mass, and in the person of the minister."[15] Is He not present in each Christian personally? St. Paul asks, "Do you not realize that Jesus Christ is in you?" (2 Cor 13:5) Indeed, we must realize how intimately and personally near He is! We have this confidence through the gift and grace of Baptism: "Christ in you, the hope of glory." (Col 1:27)

We are given the challenges and opportunities to be called into Christ in the midst of a very materialistic, hedonistic, individualistic and secular culture. The wounds and stains of these errors have left millions upon millions of God's people in confusion outside of His Church - and even within His Church these forces of darkness are not without effect. A false individualism can lead a person, for example, especially in the beginning, to see a great separation between his own religious life, and the religious life of the Church. He can see "church" as something external to himself - something composed of others, having some structure, rules and practices and so on. This is far from the truth, and this error can be deadly if held too long.

The Church is a living communion of persons, and we are made for communion. A false sense of separateness, of isolation, of individualism can keep a person from himself and from his vocation to love. Without love, without communion, without community we are dead.

There is one great and saving work of Christ, calling us into the one life and truth that is! God IS! And God, the God who is Love, calls us into the communion of persons that is life. The life-giving work of Jesus Christ is re-presented to creation and time in every liturgy of the Church. In an entirely unique and complete way He re-presents Himself, and is made present, in the liturgy of Holy Mass, the Eucharist.

In the Eucharist Christ is present differently, uniquely. In this liturgy of the Church, Christ, the Son of God, is "substantially" present to us all:

> By the consecration the transubstantiation of the bread and wine into the Body and Blood of Christ is brought about. Under the consecrated species of bread and wine Christ himself, living and glorious, is present in a true, real, and substantial manner: his Body and his Blood, with his soul and his divinity (cf.Council of Trent: DS1640; 1651).[16]

Because of this truth, the Lord Himself in the liturgy of the Eucharist is present to disciple us into life. The Eucharist is truly the source and the summit of the Christian life.[17] The Eucharist is the guiding light and the power of God for the work within, the interior liturgy.

Martha and Mary

Good work - the joyful expression of our nature, especially work within the work of Christ, our holy liturgy - is our human vocation. Work is necessary for a human person, an outward fruit of the inner being. The simple expression outwardly of the interior impulses of the heart is not simple for us, however, conflicted as we are by original sin. We so often do

not do what we will, or express the beauty we long for and
love. (i.e. Rom 7:15-23) We so often want to do good, yet
instead we sabotage our own intentions and defeat our own
desires.

The Scripture account of Martha and Mary may help focus
on the common conflict between prayer and good works.

> Now as they went on their way, he entered a village; and a
> woman named Martha received him into her house. And she
> had a sister called Mary, who sat at the Lord's feet and listened
> to his teaching. But Martha was distracted with much serving;
> and she went to him and said, "Lord, do you not care that my
> sister has left me to serve alone? Tell her then to help me."

> But the Lord answered her, "Martha, Martha, you are anxious
> and troubled about many things;

> one thing is needful. Mary has chosen the good portion, which
> shall not be taken away from her." [18]

Martha shows us the spiritual peril that can befall any
Christian who does not sufficiently nurture, and even treasure,
the interior life of prayer. Martha has fallen dangerously close
to sin, led into temptation in her distractions over much serving. Serving is good! Works on behalf of Jesus are good! Yet
Martha suggests that Jesus does not care for her, and that her
sister also is unconcerned for her. Martha goes on, in her distracted moment, to begin to dictate to Jesus what He should do
about it: He should tell Mary to help her. Martha has lost sight
of this blessed moment, with Jesus in her house so near to her.
In her distraction, she experiences herself far from Him, and
He far from her: she believes He does not care for her. This is
a most dangerous temptation for any Christian who is too
busy, even about the work of ministry.

Mary shows us the essential foundation for all ministry: an
interior life of prayer. This is the "good portion" that will not
be taken away, that will be carried into eternity in the kingdom, and that on this earth will establish true ministry upon

the foundation of authentic relationship with Christ in love. This is the one thing necessary: authentic relationship with Christ in love, which is entered in prayer. St. John Vianney has said most profoundly, "Prayer is nothing else than union with God."[19] The *Catechism* phrases it, "Christian prayer is a covenant relationship between God and man in Christ."[20] Without this saving relationship with God in Christ, apart from the One who is the source of all life and is life itself, we have no life. Apart from Him we are dead, and all our works are dead works.

<u>The great value of prayer</u>

Describing the great value of prayer is as easy and difficult as describing the value of love. How could someone explain to another the incomparable value of love? Love and prayer are invaluable, beyond price. We cannot truly live without love: love is the essence, the commandment, of life. So also we cannot live a truly human life - or speaking more specifically, a Christian life - without prayer.

The four crucial pillars of the Christian life are the creed, the sacraments, the moral life, and prayer. These crucial pillars we find affirmed in the very beginning of the Church, in the formation of the first believers following Peter's great sermon of Pentecost. "They devoted themselves to the teaching of the apostles and to fellowship, to the breaking of bread and the prayers." (Acts 2:42) These four pillars find close similarity today to the foundational four parts of the *Catechism*: part one, the profession of faith ("the teachings of the apostles"); part two, celebration of the Christian mystery (the sacraments, or "the breaking of the bread"); part three, life in Christ (Christian morality, or "fellowship"); and part four, prayer.

A building that lacks support on one of its four pillars is in serious danger; if two pillars are lacking there is certain disaster! Pushing the analogy to our Catholic faith, we can see that the analogy does have merit. Christianity today suffers from divisions and denominations, characterized by incomplete adherence to the full four pillars. Some of our Protestant brethren, for example, hold to many of the doctrines of traditional Christianity, keep a faithful moral life, seek a living prayer relationship with the Lord, and yet lack the sacramental dimension. The divisions among us hurt very seriously our witness to Christ in the world.

On the other hand, a Catholic may hold fast to the creed, participate in the sacraments, and follow the moral teachings – but he may lack a vital communion of prayer in Christ. Such a Catholic will suffer, and through him the whole Church will suffer. Prayer is the communion through which life flows in the Holy Spirit. If prayer communion is missing, life is missing; if prayer is weak or impersonal, so too is the Christian life. A man might be a powerful apologist, for example, expounding the doctrines and defending the faith with precision and clarity! Yet if this man lacks the living unction of prayer-communion in his soul, his words can fall hard, legal and lifeless from his mouth. The Gospel is a gospel of life: it is not proclaimed apart from the life of the Spirit.

It is also important to recognize that prayer alone is not sufficient! All four pillars together enable the wholeness that Christ desires and the Church needs for her apostolate. Prayer alone, without grounding in authentic doctrine, can lead away from Christ and not toward Him. There are very "spiritual" and "prayerful" heretics, who are both deceived and deceivers. We can fabricate a "Jesus" of our own preference if we stray from the revelation entrusted to the Church. Without the sacraments, we can lean toward presumption; apart from the moral teachings of the Church we can fall into a misguided sense that justifies our own wrong opinions. Many of the false teachers and new religions of our day offer "prayer" – yet outside of the way of Christ.

We need to keep in mind, then, the errors on both sides of the crucial value of prayer in Catholic life. There are temptations in some to bypass prayer altogether, or to hold prayer at a "safe" and controllable distance from their own hearts. For these Christians, prayer has stagnated as mere recitation, or merely multiplication of religious words and phrases. Prayer has never become communion for them. For these, prayer is always monologue, and has never become dialogue. There remains a profound loneliness for these Christians, who never approach the real meeting of God in prayer. For these Christians, prayer must become a new fountain of new hope! The real meaning of prayer – the real experience of prayer – the real presence of Jesus Christ in prayer – remains a treasure and a blessing yet to be found. I encourage you here, my brothers and sisters! Let us learn, and grow together.

There are others who are superficially infatuated with prayer for its own sake, who seek supernatural consolations and experiences for their own sakes. The first group appears to have not enough prayer, the second, too much! In truth, however, both of these misdirected groups have not yet entered real prayer. This second group avoids matters of doctrine as controversial, or divisive. Some minimize the importance of the sacraments, as contrary to ecumenical unity. Some are little concerned with difficult moral questions challenging the world today, as obstacles to the gospel of the unconditional love of Christ for everyone. Some replace the fullness of the Gospel with a lesser one of their own, and exhort all to an uncritical embrace of vaguely understood "prayer". Such ungrounded and self-satisfying "prayer" is spiritually dangerous, and open to satanic counterfeits. For these Christians as for the first group, I exhort you, my brothers and sisters: let us approach Him, the source of true living water, and let us drink together of this one and authentic Source.

This book considers prayer in the life of a disciple, a Catholic Christian. We will probe, and with God's grace enter, the beautiful communion of prayer offered us by Jesus in the *Our Father*. It must always be within His Church where our prayer can grow, fully and completely, to fruitful communion. Within the faithful fellowship He established in His first apostles and has preserved through His abiding Holy Spirit - the Catholic Church - here within the embrace of the Church our faith is safe, our sacramental life sure, our moral guidance true, and our life of prayer vital.

Chapter 2. Becoming Present in Prayer

Prayer and Communion

> Christian prayer is a covenant relationship between God and man in Christ. It is the action of God and of man, springing forth from both the Holy Spirit and ourselves, wholly directed to the Father, in union with the human will of the Son of God made man.[21]

We must open ourselves wide to understand prayer! For our prayer to be fully prayer, we must be personally, humanly present to God in our praying. Prayer is more than petitions, more than words, more than my expressed needs - real or felt. Prayer is a relationship of persons: the divine Persons of God - Father, Son and Holy Spirit - and human persons - you, me and all the people of God. Prayer is a relationship, and flowing within that relationship with vitality and fecundity is communication, communion, love.

Relationships among persons can be found among many possibilities. A relationship can be based on blood, on convenience, on geographical proximity, on economic advantage - it can be superficial or deep, lasting or temporary, precious or expendable. Christian prayer is a covenant relationship: a most solemn commitment and bond. God, for His part, will not break His word! God has committed Himself to this relationship! The Son, sent by the Father, has sealed the promise in His own precious blood and left us a guarantee after His resurrection and ascension, the abiding Holy Spirit. This is the eternal covenant, into which we are called through the gospel of Christ. Entering covenant relationship with Him we enter prayer.

Christian prayer is essentially bound to the communion of divine Persons of the Holy Trinity. A Christian never prays alone; a Christian never is alone. A Christian has entered saving relationship, spiritually immersed in dynamic eternal divine love, in the instant he entered Christ by faith and Baptism. We believe, if and when we do believe, into Jesus Christ. We are baptized, when we are baptized, into Jesus Christ the Son, the God-man.

In Christ, we share with Him and in Him His privileged place in the Trinity: facing His Father, now by adoption our Father, in the eternal communion of divine love in the Holy Spirit; now we have a certain participation in the prayer-out-pouring, the self-gift, the flow of love's cascading torrents between Father and Son. We share this blessed communion! We offer our humble parts in the infinite exchange. This is our prayer. This is our part, to utter in truth "our Father" through the words of Christ the Son and in Him.

This holy privilege is always, for us, privilege enabled by adoption. We can never say "Father" in the same way that the only-begotten Son says "Father". We share life in Him, in the Holy Trinity, yet He is life; He is by nature what we participate in by gift and by adoption. Yet what bliss is ours by this gift!

Prayer remains a mystery, for all the attempts of man to define or describe it. Prayer has its origin and its end in mystery, in God, and for that reason retains an impenetrable core however we try to probe into it. Christian prayer is essentially trinitarian prayer. The supreme mystery of the Christian revelation is this mystery of God as Trinity: one God, three Persons. In Christian prayer, in and through Christ the Son, we enter the divine mystery of divine love-communion enjoyed eternally in Father, Son and Holy Spirit.

Prayer is dynamic, flowing, vital. Prayer is an exchange, having in our part ebbs and flows, back and forth, giving and receiving, requiring time to grow in intensity and mature in substance. Prayer requires relationship, and enables relationship. Prayer proceeds from covenant relationship between man and God, and is the self-gift of the one to the other. In this way, prayer is the flow of grace from God to man and, with consent and self-offering, back from man to God again. Prayer, then, is grace alive, grace flowing and overflowing, sealing the covenant communion.

Grace is life, a participation in the life of God pouring forth from Him into and through His Church, empowering our return to Him, enabling our life in Him. Prayer is the exchange of grace, the giving and receiving of His life. His grace, His life flows into us and awakens that saving longing for Him. We yearn, we reach, we grasp and cry and grope in the darkness, stammering our first hopes toward Him: we pray. Our prayer is a journey, a pilgrimage to the promise. It is our return, our humble gift. He gives Himself to us; we give ourselves to Him. This is prayer.

> Likewise the Spirit helps us in our weakness; for we do not know how to pray as we ought, but the Spirit himself intercedes for us with sighs too deep for words.[22]

We do not know how to pray as we ought, but the Spirit prays within, upholding our prayer with grace and life. The Holy Spirit proceeds eternally from the Father and the Son, as Love[23], as Gift[24]. Thus it is fitting for Him to carry our prayer, to enkindle our prayer with the fire of divine communion. In Him, the Spirit, is our prayer entrusted for the Father. He who is Gift carries and enlivens our gift; He who is Love enflames our humble self-offering with that burning in our hearts hidden even from ourselves. We do not know how to pray as we ought, but His tongues of fire sweep up into a sweet oblation the sacrifice we yearn to offer.

Every gift of man is a token of the giver. We give some thing, some symbol, but through the gift we give ourselves. Every gift, then, is an offer of relationship, of covenant, of exchange. The gift of God overwhelms all our experience, reaching to the core of our understanding, penetrating to the core of our being. The gift of God is God: God indivisible, God inseparable, God always One. God is eternally and necessarily both giving and receiving; He is both loving and being loved, necessarily, within the life of the Holy Trinity. Hence also Grace must return. Grace must flow, as the living exchange of love that it is. The life of God is cast forth like seeds upon the ground, seeds that must grow to return to Him.

Our prayer begins with words, sent forth into the darkness with hope, empowered with a grace we may not even sense. We entrust these words with hope, in trembling we attach our signature daring to believe in light that cannot be seen. In time, our words deepen in meaning, the meaning of a person, the meaning of myself. My words become me, and His listening becomes His presence and promise, so close even in the darkness of prayer. My words, enlivened by His grace, carrying in meaning my heart, myself, become my presentation to Him, my self-offering. Even here, in the beginning, prayer is the exchange of grace in covenant relationship. Yet this is only the beginning: relationship grows, requiring time. Communion deepens in time, unfolding in intimacy and fullness of self-gift.

We will see that our prayer is intended by God to deepen, grow and unfold in time to include much in prayer-relationship that we cannot know in the beginning. Our life of prayer begins with vocal prayer, and is intended to develop toward more and more authentic personal relationship with God, person to Persons. Yet our prayer will never outgrow vocal prayer! The *Our Father* will show us this, giving us as it does, stage by stage in the entire developing life of prayer, the most crucial vocal petition one stage at a time that is appropriate for us.

Some Difficulties with a Formula Vocal Prayer

The *Our Father* is the foundation for all prayer. It is a simple vocal prayer, taught to children and memorized by millions. Because it is so simple, so well known and familiar, it can be recited with no real personal engagement whatsoever. We can pray this prayer with the detachment of a tape recorder set on "play": the words are coming out and filling the air, but without the full participation of a human mind and heart.

We can recite this prayer too easily. All appearances would show we are praying to God, yet within ourselves we can be a million miles away, remembering this or that, planning this or that, dreaming or wishing, regretting or reliving some past moment among the many that seem to be slipping through our fingers.

Vocal prayer, including this most important of formula prayers of the Church, requires both attention and devotion to be a full, meaningful human act. We should not be mindless or distracted when in prayer to God! Ironically in this prayer, the *Our Father*, distraction is too easy and too common. We know this prayer too well! We have recited it too long, for so many years! We so often recite it together in groups, with a certain speed and rhythm that does not allow reflection or consideration, so that we have learned to merely recite it and not pray it.

This prayer is a treasure. It hides within its simplicity a pearl of great price, a dynamo of spiritual power, a furnace of transforming love. This prayer can change us, forming and reforming, healing and enabling, directing us toward the only goal that a human person must seek, to fully live his life. God has not hidden this from us! He did not give us this treasure in some language we could not translate, or accessible only by the highly educated or brilliant, requiring wealth or sophistication. This prayer is most simple and plain, poor in words yet opening into the riches of divine wisdom. It is so like our God, who guards a special love for the poor, and who entrusts Himself not to the wise and understanding but to little ones.

God enfolded into this prayer all that there is of prayer. It is the complete prayer, and even more. The *Our Father* is more than we commonly mean by the word "prayer", because commonly we do not understand prayer. Prayer is nothing else than union with God, as St. John Vianney has said. Prayer is union with God! This is so simple yet profound. Commonly we understand prayer as precisely separation from God! Often our prayers are cries to Him as one distant and separated. We ask for His presence, His love, His mercy, His gifts - as though He were far away from our problems and hungers, our needs and hopes. Yet He is closer than our breathing, or the beating of our hearts. He is holding us, with us even as we call out to Him. He is upholding us and infusing us, even as we cry for His help.

The first step in unfolding this prayer is to begin again to pray it. We must renew our prayer, praying with the attention and devotion required of vocal prayer, and deserved by God with whom we pray.

Attention in prayer means attentiveness to whom we pray, attentiveness to who is praying, and attentiveness to what is prayed. I need the sound basis of humble self-knowledge; I need the realization that I stand before God the almighty and eternal, my creator and redeemer. I need to offer my words and actions, my intentions, my life, aware of all these things as they come forward in my prayer with God. In other words, prayer from my side is a human act, the act of a human person who is conscious and engaged and honestly present as person in the action. Prayer cannot be an automatic, disengaged recital - in prayer it must be I myself speaking, offering, inviting, giving. Prayer insists upon my presence! I cannot counterfeit prayer with mere external appearances! Prayer requires recollection: the regathering and refocusing in reality. Here I am, before God. Prayer, like love, demands the attentive heart.

Devotion is the authentic human response, in heart and will, to the realizations of authentic attention. Reverence is awakened by the realizations of this moment of prayer: the presence of God, the humble offerings I bring, the poor words I dare to speak before Him. Reverence finds an active component in the human will, a center of warm response to truth and vocation, which is devotion. A desire to respond in truth is awakened in authentic prayer, yet this desire must be approved and affirmed in the heart. There must be a resolution, an intention, a "yes" that is only appropriate to the truth and presence of God. This is devotion, a "yes" surging up within the human heart that summons the whole person to obedience in the truth of this moment - a moment of prayer, yet a moment meant to remain.

In attention, the mind is engaged in communion with God. In devotion, the heart is turned to face Him, and beholding Him, even though poorly and even through the mists that seem almost impenetrable in the beginning - knowing His presence the soul finds rest.

In prayer, if we want and value this, our prayer can grow both in attention and in devotion. With the prayer, the *Our Father*, a definite intention is required because of years possibly of bad habit - perhaps years of mere habitual recitation and mindless repetition. Yet this prayer, the *Our Father*, has potency within itself that deserves to be known. Once we begin really to hear this prayer, we discover its power. As we learn to cooperate with the power - the grace - awaiting within, we discover ourselves anew, enflamed with a share in the passion of God. This prayer is a symphony of goodness and wisdom, even in the simplicity of its common words and form.

How then are we to pray this prayer? To begin with, we must approach this prayer as the gift it is: a gift from the mouth of Jesus Himself. This prayer is a uniquely significant prayer, yet all prayer must be approached reverently as communication with God, as dialogue with Him. In the beginning it may seem that our prayer is only monologue, that only I am talking and I do not know whether anyone is listening. Here, the faith of the Church is needed even when our own faith seems very weak indeed. The Church assures us that God is present, and He is listening. Saints throughout the ages assure us that He is with us, that He is near, that He hears us and in His own way will answer. All true prayer is in fact dialogue, even when we cannot hear Him.

In the beginning, then, we must hold fast with faith as we pray, if not our own faith then trust in the faith of the Church. Our own faith begins weak and small, the weakness and smallness of a child - yet a child is strong in the strength of his parents. We hold fast in the faith of the Church, trusting her as the child trusts his mother, trusting the words she teaches and the love behind the words. So too we pray this prayer, believing it is true yet understanding very little of what we are saying. Understanding will grow: the child will grow. Our prayer will unfold; the intentions in the petitions of this prayer will be understood with time. The rich meaning still veiled in the interior dimensions of this divine gift, the *Our Father*, will come forth like fruit in due season to the farmer who patiently tends the garden. We approach this prayer, then, with trust and with patience.

We must approach this prayer, and all prayer, with reverence - yet reverence also is a virtue developed in time through grace and human cooperation with grace. Sadly, we live in an irreverent culture, with lack of regard for the holy and lack of respect for human persons. We as a culture are infected with irreverence as we are with impatience and unbelief. Yet grace is light poured into such darkness, revealing gradually the presence of the divine so near to us, and even within us and others. Grace abounding upon grace grows as the interior life grows, exposing the sin hiding and lurking in darkness, and illuminating the world of miracles around us, and opening our eyes to see the radiant splendor of Christ present and within and among His people.

Reverence clothes the soul as it grows in the interior life of prayer, putting upon it the habit of virtue. Virtues such as humility and faith, hope and patience, magnanimity and charity are fed through the interior communion enabled in prayer. In the beginning, we hold fast to the gift of this prayer with trust in mother Church, with the small seed of faith that we treasure, with hope in the One still hidden and unseen, with a love only beginning to be experienced.

Chapter 3. Prayer in the Interior Liturgy

The Mysterious and Perfect Sequence of Petitions

St. Thomas saw two remarkable truths in the seven petitions of the *Our Father*:

Now in the Lord's Prayer not only do we ask for all that we may rightly desire, but also in the order wherein we ought to desire them, so that this prayer not only teaches us to ask, but also directs all our affections. Thus it is evident that the first thing to be the object of our desire is the end, and afterwards whatever is directed to the end.[25]

St. Thomas saw, then, that 1) the seven petitions contain in some way all the legitimate desires we could have, and 2) the sequence of the petitions, as Jesus gave them to us, is highly significant. He gave us the order in which we ought to desire these gifts, for our affections to be properly related and directed.

The sequence of the petitions, then, gives us from first to last what should be loved and desired and sought in our prayer, in proper order. To attain communion with "our Father who art in heaven", we must first desire the holiness of His name. Then, next in order of affection, we should love and desire and seek the coming of the kingdom. Next in the order of affection we should desire and love and seek the doing of His will on earth as in heaven - and so on through the rest of the prayer.

St. Thomas helps us to understand a great truth of the *Our Father* - the mystery of the sequence of the seven petitions of the prayer. Any one or two petitions from the sequence could well be isolated and taken into personal prayer! Any one or two of the petitions could serve as objects for meditation and reflection, and beautifully, fruitfully so. Each and any of the seven facets of this precious diamond of a prayer can channel the light of God into our souls, for great benefit. Yet these seven petitions in particular form a divinely given completeness. These seven petitions in the divinely given sequence and ordering that they have in the *Our Father*, give to every person the directions of a spiritual journey that God Himself, in Christ, reveals to us. The *Our Father* explains the journey of faith to every person.

The descent of grace and the ascent of discipleship

As Jesus teaches this prayer to us today, we might imagine Him when He first taught it, during His "Sermon on the Mount"[26], at the summit of a high hill or mountain, surrounded by many listeners below Him. Jesus was standing there at the summit of a mount geographically, as He was standing interiorly at the summit of the spiritual mount, in ever-present communion with His Father. Below Him then geographically and spiritually were the crowds, listening, hungry for truth, and in their own hearts longing for the blessed communion with God for which they were made. In this context Jesus teaches the *Our Father*.

Jesus, with His teaching, is casting a great net out to the crowds. He stands in holy and interior communion with the Father, looking upon the people, and He casts out to the farthest reaches of their darkness, confusion and longing. He casts out His saving truth to the extremes of these, His beloved sheep; to the darkest corners where His little and lost ones stumble. Jesus reaches outward in His love from where He is, in the intimate communion of the Holy Trinity, to where His people languish in the deadly clutches of the evil one.

Jesus calls us all from wherever we are, to where He is. Jesus invites us all, wherever we stand in relation to Him, to receive His saving grace, to drink of His living water, to hear His words of truth - to come. He invites us all to come. Streaming from His Sacred Heart is the enabling and empowering grace that will allow us, no matter how far away we stand, to come.

The grace pouring forth from the divine fount of His human heart, so to speak, then flows from His mouth to carry saving truth in the words of this remarkable prayer, the *Our Father*. His grace is out-poured from where He is, calling us to Himself, that where He is we might be also: we, who even now might be wounded and hurting, crippled and dehumanized, paralyzed in fears and locked in bondage to the dark powers of the evil one.

His grace descends to us through the seven petitions. He calls us to Himself, to come to Him there before the Father! Yet we are so far away, and the journey is not one step, it is seven. The mountain of our pilgrimage, to Him there at the summit, is a hard road - yet it is easier than the futility of human life apart from Him.

This mountain has, as it were, seven plateaus or resting stations where we may pause and find nourishment. There are seven stations where He provides for us who journey to Him. In this journey, which is the pilgrimage offered to every human person, Christ provides for us in particular and appropriate ways, at each of the seven stations.

At each of the seven stations of this mountain of ascent, there is grace and there is prayer. At each station of this great in-gathering which is the saving work of Christ, there is our cry to Him in prayer, and there is His loving response in grace. The work of Christ within the soul, the interior liturgy, thus is a work of seven stations. Each station has its appropriate prayer, and each station has grace from God appropriate to the station. Each station as well has its right and appropriate response within the soul, within the whole person, to its particular and enabling grace from God.

This pattern of prayer to God, and grace from God, and

rightful human response is to be folded into all of our Catholic life. In our ascent to God, in the interior liturgy of Christ at work in our souls, this pattern of prayer and grace and response is found at each of the seven stations.

Grace descends. Grace descends that we might ascend, as the Son descended that He might also ascend (Eph 4:7-10). Grace has its origin in God, the Holy Trinity: a grace received is our human participation in this divine Trinitarian life. Grace descends from its fount in the Sacred Heart of Jesus, the Son, who stands before the Father in the eternal communion of love, and it descends through the stages of our estrangement from Him, step by step, station by station. The saving grace of God descends to us in His condescending love, His willing *kenosis* (see Addendum p. 224), His unreserved Self-gift. Grace reaches down to us where we are, where we all begin at first: lost in darkness and bewildered in sin. Grace reaches down even to you or me, as a wandering and lost sheep (Lk 15: 4), as a lost coin (Lk 15: 8), to give us freedom from the treacherous grasp of evil.

His grace descends in stages, or steps – through the plateaus of the mountain of ascent, or through the stations of the saving interior liturgy – in condescending love and meas-ured grace, that He might not overwhelm us in His glory, or discourage us in our return to Him. Instead, each of the sta-tions has its prayer, its grace, and its proper response in us.

In the plan of God, in the beautiful pattern of the *Our Father*, God gives us the course we are to follow. He gives us, at each station, the petition most necessary, for the grace most needed, to direct us to respond as we should toward our final goal in Him.

The grace that draws us

To where are we directed, in our proper response within

His saving work? We are always directed to ascend, through the grace descending, to Christ awaiting in the next station ahead. Thus the grace flows down to us, station by station, petition by petition, descending from its source in God our hope and our goal. Thus we ascend, station by station, beginning at the base of the mountain, so to speak, seeking always to ascend to where He is. As we ascend, if we ascend, the saving grace at each station is God's answer to the petition He gave us to pray there, and we are directed ever upward, to the next station awaiting us.

Thus we can comprehend, and perhaps extend, the understanding of St. Thomas Aquinas regarding the mystery of the sequence of the seven petitions. If first is the desire, and next is what is directed toward the desire, then we see the seven petitions as we pray them as the proper hierarchy of desire, if we would rightly seek union with God. Since, however, first is the desire and next is what is directed toward the desire, we see that the very last of the seven petitions is the very first step needed to become directed toward our final desire in God. The last of the petitions is the first station of the liturgy, the place of the first of the plateaus along the mountain of ascent. The journey begins at the end of the prayer, and is directed step by step, station by station, petition by petition in return to the source of our prayer in Jesus Christ. Together with Him and in Him, we ascend in His grace, that we might finally in Him declare in joy, in beatific vision, "Our Father, who art in heaven!"

The prayer *Our Father* prepares a way through the wilderness within the soul confused in sin - a way made straight for Him. Grace then can flow through this way, this path made straight, petition by petition from the first and primary desire for the holiness of the divine name, through the pilgrimage of petitions down to the last. The *Our Father*, like John the Baptist, prepares the way of the Lord, making His path straight.

The journey of a disciple begins with that first deliverance from evil, when by grace freedom is first hoped for and in part experienced. Deliverance from evil frees the soul, and directs the soul toward the interior discernment enabled by temptation. Faithfulness through temptation then leads the soul to the encounter with God's mercy: forgiveness as we forgive others. Embracing mercy with justice, we hunger to approach the altar on which is offered our daily bread. There at the altar, which is the cross, we are given an understanding of His will on earth as it is in heaven. Embracing this will, we pray for His kingdom; receiving the good news of the kingdom, we long for the holiness of the name. Entering the holiness of the name, we behold the Father who is in heaven, in His only-begotten Son in the unity of the Holy Spirit.

This journey - an interior journey within the soul, guided by grace and illuminated by the seven petitions of the *Our Father*, is illustrated in figure 1 (page 43). In this figure, a picture is presented that suggests "shells," or layers of mansions in the soul surrounding the center where His Majesty dwells, as seen by Teresa of Jesus (of Avila). The journey presented in this book is reminiscent of that seen by Teresa, the one journey that is our common vocation. Here, however, the journey is seen in terms of this interior liturgy, guided by this most beautiful prayer-treasure, given us by His Majesty Himself.

The unfolding of love

The interior liturgy is, first and last, a liturgy of love. It is a work of God come down from heaven to men, to gather us into the saving love of God. The way that love develops in us, the way that love grows and matures by grace as a result of the work of Christ, has been recognized in the Church for centuries. The life of Christ develops in a human person in stages.

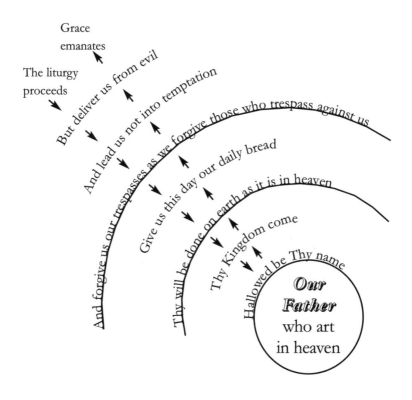

Figure 1: Petitions of the Interior Liturgy

The interior liturgy proceeds through the seven stations of the prayer, each with its particular petition. Grace emanates from the center, where awaits, so to speak, Our Father in heaven. We begin from the outside, drawn and empowered by His emanating grace, and journey to the center, station by station and petition by petition. The journey is ever more inward, ever more interior - yet also, ever higher to where the Lord our God dwells.

The two Dark Nights are indicated by the solid arcs.

St Bernard of Clairvaux wrote, in the twelfth century, of the degrees of charity through which we must pass, if love is to grow to fullness in us. These degrees of love define the stages of the interior life of a person: His life in us. These degrees of love, these stages of the interior life, are the unfolding of the liturgy of Christ in the soul of a human person. The interior liturgy is most simply explained using the language and terms of love – the love that Christ works in us. The language of love fulfilled is dialogue, an exchange of person with person. At first God gives, out of the infinite mercy of His love, yet He gives to invite the response of love.

In the first movement of the interior liturgy, there is by the grace of Christ a love toward God that is based upon gratitude, yet remains effectively self-centered: We love God because of the great good that He has done and can do for us. Love, however, has begun! Through the petitions of the stations of the first movement of the interior liturgy, God works His beginnings of love. We pray first for deliverance from evil, then for overcoming of temptation, and then for forgiveness of our sin – and God grants us all this and more. We rejoice in this great saving power of God in our lives, and well we should! This marks the beginning of charity in us, and the first movement of the saving work of the Lord.

The third petition of our prayer is more than, "forgive us our trespasses." It is the second part of that third petition, "as we forgive those who trespass against us," that invites the mystical intervention known as the dark night of the senses – the first dark night of the soul, of St. John of the Cross. The conditional "as we forgive" calls down a work of God in the soul to open our hearts to mercy. Charity requires this mercy! We are called to be not merely grateful receivers of love from God, but living agents of His saving love as well. We are called to live the divine image, both giving and receiving mercy in love. A work is required in us, therefore, to carve out within our hearts a giving softness and a patient love - mercy, toward those who hurt us.

"As we forgive" then initiates the second great movement of God's saving work - the second movement of the interior liturgy - by calling forth the dark trials of the first "night" described by John of the Cross. For the person persevering through this trial, there awaits on the other side a bright new day of the Christian life, a new consecration, a second conversion, the illuminative stage of the soul. In this movement of the liturgy, the person enters a new experience of charity - a new "degree" in the language of St. Bernard. In this deeper, more mature and more fully personal relationship with God, we begin to love Him not only for the good that He can do and has done for us - beyond that, we begin to love Him because of the splendor, the glory, the beauty of God as He is in Himself. We begin to love God because of who God is - not merely because of the good that He can do for us.

In this second great movement of the interior liturgy, the new dimension of charity awakened in the soul has expression in our relationships with other human persons also. The two great commandments are always linked! Our love for God always is linked with our love for neighbor. We cannot in truth claim to love God if we have no love for our neighbor. In this movement of the liturgy, our love for neighbor finds a new dimension also, along with our greatly elevated love for God. We are enabled to begin to see, for this is an unfolding process, other persons as God sees them. We begin to see others in the light of God; we begin to see their great dignity and importance to Him. Our neighbors therefore begin to have this divinely grounded importance for us personally. The dignity and beauty of every living person begins to be revealed to us, in our own eyes, because we see them in His light. This wholly new dimension of charity is the work of God in the soul, in the interior liturgy, in the second major movement of consecration at the altar.

In this movement, our need is expressed in petition for our daily bread - the bread from heaven which sustains and nurtures the Christian life - and for our ability to truly do the will of God on earth. These are the fourth and fifth stations of the liturgy, prayed in the next two petitions of the *Our Father*.

Divine charity has found new heights in this movement, but it is not yet perfected. There still remain traces of self-centeredness that require a deeper work of God in the soul. This deeper work, this more penetrating purification, is known as the dark night of the spirit, in the theology of St. John of the Cross. This purging darkness is invited into the soul through the second part of the petition of the fifth station, "...as it is in heaven." When the soul hungers for His will to be done on earth even in the purity and glory of that perfect obedience of heaven, then the soul is ready for the final purgation possible on earth before death itself: the purgation that St. John of the Cross has termed the dark night of the spirit.

In the dark aridity of this second night, the soul is being finally prepared for the fullness of communion with God, and of collaboration with God in His saving work. The third movement of the interior liturgy is the movement of most authentic embrace - the most intimate, personal and complete of the stages of growing union with God in love. This is called the unitive stage, or the stage of the perfect, in traditional Catholic spirituality. This is the final movement of the liturgy, the communion of persons with and in the divine Persons. This is the perfection of charity, in which God is genuinely loved because of who He is: He is God, holy of holies, lord of lords and king of kings. He is God over all, most splendid and beautiful and true. And in Him only do we find ourselves, or know ourselves, or love ourselves; in Him only do we love any other. In Him only do we see, and love our neighbor. In Him is all, and He is our all.

In this third movement of the interior liturgy, our charity finds its full development: the development unto fruitfulness. The petitions of the stations of the liturgy here are the two: thy kingdom come, and hallowed be thy name. These petitions form the final gathering into the fullness of the exclamation which expresses our deepest heart-desire: the loving communion with God the Holy Trinity.

To summarize: the interior liturgy is most simply revealed as the developing work of charity in the soul. The stages of this love are the stages of the spiritual life of traditional Catholic understanding.

The stage of the beginner is the purgative stage, in which the soul loves God and others selfishly. In this stage the soul must guard, protect and nurture the charity received, lest it be lost through sin or neglect. This stage of the soul is the work of the first movement of the interior liturgy, prayed in three stations. The petitions of these three stations are first, "deliver us from evil," then second, "lead us not into temptation," then third, "forgive us our trespasses as we forgive those who trespass against us." The last part of this last petition, "as we forgive those who trespass against us," is the prayer of entry into the first dark night: the dark night of the senses. This dark night is the first passive purgation from God in the soul, and is the preparation for the great gift of infused contemplation in the illuminative stage of the spiritual life.

The stage of the proficient is the illuminative stage, in which the person begins to love God because of who He is, yet still with traces of mercenary self-interest. In this stage the soul must seek to grow in the life of charity, of good works. This stage of the soul is the work of the second movement of the interior liturgy, prayed in two stations. The petitions of these two stations are the fourth, "give us this day our daily bread," and the fifth, "thy will be done on earth as it is in heaven." The last part of this fifth petition, "(thy will be done) as it is in heaven," is the prayer of entry into the second dark night: the dark night of the spirit. This dark night is the final passive purgation from God in the soul before death itself, and is the preparation for the great gift of union in the unitive stage of the spiritual life.

The stage of the perfect is the unitive stage, in which the soul seeks to remain in Him, bearing the beautiful fruit of this union. In this stage the soul seeks to remain in the union of prayer, and in the life of charity and good works. This stage of the soul is the work of the third movement of the interior liturgy, prayed in two stations. The petitions of these two stations are the sixth, "thy kingdom come," and the seventh, "hallowed be thy name." The invocation of this last petition of the liturgy, which is the first petition of the prayer the *Our Father*, "hallowed be thy name," is the preparation for entry into the blessed presence of God, for beholding His divine face. In Christ the Son, has been revealed a great mystery: the mystery of His name. In the Son we stand to see the face of the Father, in the bliss of their Spirit. Here we say, "our Father, who art in heaven!"

The Interior Liturgy

The *Our Father* is the rite of the interior liturgy - the rubrics through which we move interiorly and then exteriorly in free response to the great and saving work of God in Christ. A liturgy is a work of the Church in communion with Christ, a celebration and enactment of His Paschal mystery, expressed in all the sacramental liturgies and especially in the liturgy of the Eucharist. The liturgy of the Church is the great and saving work of Christ continued, and made present in the world. All liturgies of the Church, celebrated in community, call forth the personal contribution and participation of each member present, to join in the work of Christ.

All liturgies communally celebrated have then a resonance within each person present: all are called to full participation, to be true co-laborers with Him. All communal liturgies resonate within each person present through the interior liturgy in the soul of the person. Christ works in the Church through her liturgies; Christ works in the person through the interior liturgy within the soul – a liturgy moving through definite parts in the whole. In the interior liturgy, seen in the light of the communal liturgy of the Church, we see the fullness of collaboration.

The interior liturgy has three main parts, as does the liturgy of the Church. We can see this in the rites of the Liturgy of the Eucharist. There is the first part, the liturgy of the Word; the second part, the consecration at the altar; the third part, the holy communion. So also the interior liturgy, directed by the prayer given us by Jesus, follows these three main parts:

First, The Liturgy of the Word:

1.   Deliver us from evil.

2.   Lead us not into temptation.

3.   Forgive us our trespasses as we forgive those who trespass against us.

Second, The Consecration at the Altar:

4.   Give us this day our daily bread.

5.   Thy will be done on earth as it is in heaven.

Third, The Holy Communion:

6.   Thy kingdom come.

7.   Hallowed be thy name.

We will see how these prayers of the interior liturgy develop in the life of the Christian, how they form us in Christ and form us to be heart-priests in Christ. We will see how these prayers gather us first into asceticism and self-knowledge, then uncover our needs – and open our souls – for dark nights of purgation that prepare us for the transforming gift of mystical prayer, or contemplation, bearing fruit in Christian lives of virtue and holiness.

Mary and Prayer

The work of Christ in the human soul is ordered toward our regathering, our healing, our restoration. It does not always seem that way! We experience struggle in our journey of following Jesus, and times of darkness and confusion. Always close to us, always ready to help along the way, is Mary the mother of Jesus. Jesus Christ our Lord is true God and true man – He is like us in all ways but sin[27]. We, however, are not and cannot be like Him: a divine Person. We are invited into a certain participation, a share in His life and His nature – yet always by participation only. Mary, however, like each of us is fully a human person, not divine. She was redeemed by the Self-sacrifice of Jesus, as we were. She is saved through grace, as we are. Mary shows us, through her ever-willing "yes" to God, the most beautiful and most complete human worship of God. We will find, along this journey together, a most beautiful help and true companion in Mary.

As we approach Jesus in our prayer, especially through this prayer that He gave us, the *Our Father*, we find Mary always near. The rightful place of Mary in the life of Christians deserves volumes upon volumes! In this book, the role of Mary will be considered in more detail later, in particular encounters of the interior liturgy. Yet even here, beginning to consider the "yes" that God yearns to hear from each human heart and life, how can we neglect to honor Mary who pronounced this word with such simplicity and clarity and consistency? The Church honors Mary in the prayer, the *Hail Mary*, and in the devotion of the rosary with its beautiful meditations upon the mysteries of the faith. The icons of the Church, and especially of the Eastern rites of the Church, are beautiful windows opening to the divine. Mary is in a sense an icon for us – an icon of the human obedience of love – yet she is more than a mere icon! Mary lives today as mother for us, each and all, mother of the complete Christ. The *Our Father*, together with the *Hail Mary* and the *Glory Be*, intertwined as they are in the rosary, become windows into the great mysteries of the faith, all together working the saving work of Christ in the heart of the believer. But here, in this book, we will focus only on the great prayer the *Our Father*!

Mary is mother for all Christians, and our personal motherly companion in Christ, in the interior life. At the beginning of our interior life Mary may not be recognized by us as having the importance she actually has! Among the saints she is the most humble and most quiet, and even in many Catholics who grew up with traditional Marian devotion, her true place remains in a sense a hidden mystery.

Our relationship with Mary, in the spiritual life, usually parallels our relationship with Jesus. If our relationship with Jesus is formal and impersonal, then probably our relationship with Mary is also. If our relationship with Mary is superficial, probably our relationship with Jesus is superficial too. As we come into a more personal, authentic and loving relationship with Jesus, most probably we enter as well into a real bond with His mother. As our union with Christ the Son grows toward that intimate relation of the unitive stage, the move-

ment of communion, so also does our communion embrace all
the people of God, and preeminently His holy mother Mary.
There may be exceptions to this rule, but they are the exceptions, not the norm, due to extraordinary situations such as dis-
torted formation, erroneous prejudices and misinformation.

In the beginning of the interior liturgy, and the spiritual
life, it is as difficult to know Mary rightly as it is to know Jesus
rightly. The mystery of who Jesus is was obscure to all, including His close disciples, through the entire earthly ministry
before the cross. The brief insights gained by some, notably
Peter, before that defining crisis, were due to the intervening
grace of the Father, and would vanish into vapor when Jesus
was arrested. So too an understanding of the Blessed Mother
was cloaked before the cross. Indeed, the whole identity of
Mary is so closely linked to her vocation as mother of Jesus,
that we cannot understand one properly without the other.

Jesus gave a teaching during His earthly ministry to clari-
fy the honor due to Mary, but it remains largely misunder-
stood. He had just given a strong warning concerning the need
for union with Him in His work. Jesus said, "He who is not
with me is against me, and he who does not gather with me
scatters." (Lk 11:23) Then a woman in the crowd, in praise of
Mary perhaps because this woman thought that surely His
mother would be one in union with Him, said to Him, "Blessed
is the womb that bore you, and the breasts that you sucked!" In
a response that can lead to misinterpretation even today, Jesus
corrected her: "Blessed rather are those who hear the word of
God and keep it!" (Lk 11:27-28) The great honor due Mary is
not because of her role as physical mother of a remarkable
teacher, but rather because of her singular, total, faithful and
loving obedience to God. It was this obedience, her unique and
consistent "yes" to Him, enabled through the singular grace
that was given her, that obliges the whole world, and "all gen-

erations" to call her "blessed." (Lk 1:48)

In the second movement of the interior liturgy, in the liturgy of consecration at the altar, the soul is illuminated with divine light to begin to unveil the meaning and identity both of the Christ and of His mother. It is under the cross, in the patient and faithful gaze upon Him the crucified one, that we hear the revealing words, "Behold, your mother." (Jn 19:27) There begins our looking upon Mary in a new way, a way enabled in the shadow of the cross and its suffering, but also the way illuminated by a new encounter with the Holy Spirit. In the second movement of the interior liturgy and in the third, the Holy Spirit comes anew, to usher in the new work of God, and the new relationship of prayer-communion, the prayer of contemplation. In this new dialogue of prayer, Mary comes as mother, as queen, as apostle.

Prayer and Suffering

Self-offering and suffering are essential elements of prayer. Whenever love enters the place where sin remains, there will be suffering. Love in the midst of sin will always bring forth suffering. There will be suffering for the one who brings love, and there will be an invitation into suffering for the one who is loved. For both the one who loves, and the one who is loved, this suffering is a participation in the cross of Christ who suffered completely, because He loved completely. Authentic prayer will always bear suffering, because prayer is a communion of love.

Love seeks communion, and is communion. Sin is separation, and seeks separation. When communion is sought among those who seek separation, there will be suffering. We were made for communion with God and with one another, but we are born in sin and in confusion: we do not know how to be who we are. In our confusion we build with one hand and tear down with the other; we draw together and fight with one another. We seek love, but then sabotage the beloved. We lay ambushes for the beloved and for ourselves, betraying the very communion we long for so deeply.

Love and sin will not coexist: either love will overcome sin, and bring forgiveness, or sin will overcome love, and destroy it. This is the great battle of prayer: the conflict between love and sin. This is also the great battle of the mission of Christ, and the whole of evangelization. Sin is at war with love, and love is willing to suffer.

The suffering of love - the suffering of prayer - is first felt in the disciple because of his own sin. If he perseveres in faith, and grows in prayer, his suffering will expand to begin to include suffering due to the sin of others. As he grows in Christ, his suffering grows to more and more resemble the suffering of Christ, and so therefore grows in beauty, and meaning, and value. These are stages of suffering, and correspond to the stages of prayer - the stages of communion and of love in Christ.

At the beginning of our life of prayer, we struggle against the sin in our hearts, which are as rocks hardened against the truth of God. We are called to repentance, to conversion, to change: we must turn away from these sins, and make the way straight for the Way, Jesus Christ. This is the first stage of our life of prayer, the stage of ascetical prayer, the purgative way of the beginning disciple.

If we persevere in prayer and in faithfulness to the truth we know, struggling against temptations and selfishness in favor of the love of Christ, we may receive from God His great Gift. The Gift was always there, given in the very beginning, but He remained silent and unrecognized. The Holy Spirit is with us, given in Baptism, but He begins to make Himself uniquely known in the second stage of the life of prayer. In the illuminative stage, He illuminates the truth of God in the soul of the disciple: He illuminates Christ in the light He deserves as Son. In this stage of prayer, the disciple is offered the Gift; the covenant relationship with God in Christ is bathed in a light mystical and undeniable: prayer unfolds into contemplation.

Even in the stage of ascetical prayer we are offered a part in the cross of Christ! Even in the very beginning, struggling against the sin so heavy in our own hearts, the suffering we accept and endure is a blessed kiss from His passion. But in the illuminative stage, in the growing intimacy of our communion, in the light of contemplation, we are taught anew and more deeply the mystery of the cross.

Standing newly close to our mother Mary, standing in the person of the disciple beloved by Jesus, our prayer at the foot of the cross finds new resonances in His prayer, in His dialogue of love. His Sacred Heart itself is illuminated in the light of the Gift; His divine love-communion with the Father becomes the prayer of our own hearts; His divine self-offering on that coarse and bloody altar becomes, strangely, an invitation and a vocation for us as well. Our suffering, our part in the cross of Christ, now takes on the dimension not only of gift received, but also of gift given. Our suffering now is mixed: we battle against the love of this world still rooted in our hearts, and we join in the battle of intercession for His people.

The mixture of this love judges us! We cannot escape suffering: everyone born into this world will die. But there, at the foot of the cross of Christ, we look to the right and to the left: two thieves crucified beside Him show us the choices we might make - the choices open to every one of us who has been a thief. One thief seeks to hold onto his life in this world, even to the disdain of God. The other thief lets go of this life, accepts the penalty laid upon him, and trusts the suffering Christ beside him.

The mixtures of love in the second stage of the life of prayer - the incompatible mixtures, the contradictions - these God deals with in our sufferings, these fruitless thorns God uproots in the battles and the sufferings of the heart. These God extracts, and burns in the furnace of His own Sacred Heart.

The sufferings of the third stage of the life of prayer remain bound to sin and due to love, as sufferings always are so bound and so due. The sufferings of the third stage need not be spent, however, in the struggles against demons without and temptations within. They need not be wasted on the mixed witness of mercenary love. The sufferings of the third stage bring growth from the good ground, bearing fruit whether a hundredfold or sixty or thirty. The sufferings of the third stage draw the precious sap from deep within the vine, through branches now trained to abide in Him, bringing forth fruit that will remain. The sufferings of the third stage make up what is lacking in the cross of Christ, offered in union with Him, a share in His own Gift.

The sufferings of these three stages become part of our offerings, our self-gift, in the liturgy. These sufferings are intimately bonded with the work of God within us - in the interior liturgy, in the communion of our prayer in Him - and in the communal liturgy of the Holy Mass. In the Liturgy of the Word we are called to the cross; in the consecration at the altar we embrace the cross; in the Holy Communion we find communion through the cross with our Lord and Savior. In the interior liturgy our suffering is wed to His, compassionately, gradually, that we may be "heirs of God and fellow heirs with Christ, provided we suffer with him in order that we may also be glorified with him." (Rom. 8:17)

Chapter 4. Characteristics of The Our Father

The Normative Prayer

The *Our Father* is the norm of all prayer. When we try to judge our prayer life, to assess the content and intention of our own prayers, we have a sure standard and reference in the *Our Father.* Jesus said, "Pray then like this ...." We know from Jesus, in the gift of this prayer, what is to be included in prayer that is pleasing and right in the sight of God. How are we to pray? We are to pray "like this."

A standard, a norm, is effective as such only if we know how to use it. We must see as deeply as possible into this prayer, penetrating into its meaning as fully as we can. We must hear and understand as precisely as possible, exactly what is said in this prayer. We must learn what is to be included in valid petition of God, and what is not. What does He desire us to seek, and what to avoid seeking? What should we yearn for; what should we ask for? He said that whatever we ask in His name, He will give to us! What is rightly desired in His name? Ask, seek, knock He said. We need to learn as disciples what is proper for us to ask and to seek.

In this prayer, St. Thomas Aquinas wrote, we learn not only all the true goods we should rightly ask for, but the order in which we should desire these goods[28]. Later in the book we will investigate more carefully, and in some detail, the importance of the sequence of the seven petitions of the prayer. For now we listen to the wholeness, the completeness of the content itself. This prayer is complete, and so qualifies as the norm of our prayer.

This prayer is normative also because, given us by the Son, it is completely trustworthy. In our prayer to God, it is true to say that we pray, yet also it is the Holy Spirit who prays with-

in us[29]. This is especially consoling in the prayers from our
darkness and desert emptiness, when we don't know how to
pray as we ought: the Holy Spirit prays in us and intercedes for
us. (Rom. 8:26) This prayer, the *Our Father*, is ever near us
whether we wait in darkness or light, whether in desert emptiness or garden fruitfulness. It is ours, in memory; it awaits us in
the heart. The *Our Father* is our true prayer; it is the true
prayer given us by God the Son, prayed through God the Holy
Spirit, prayed to God the Father.

For a prayer to really serve as a norm, it must be held so
closely in the heart that it is always present as we pray. Our
prayer certainly is not restricted to the 54 words of the *Our
Father!* Jesus gave us not a mere formula to repeat again and
again as we pray. He gave us a formula always to be there for
us, it is true. Even when we cannot put together two words of
prayer by ourselves, so barren might we be in a night of pierc-
ing darkness and anguish, yet we are given this treasure so easily kept in memory that always it is there for us to return in
hope to our God. For this reason alone we must guard this
prayer in our hearts. It is an imperishable treasure.

In the ordinary times of our lives as well, however, the
Our Father remains normative for our whole life of prayer.
When we can pray, whether in prayer of supplication or
thanksgiving, petition or praise, whether in anguish or joy, in
confident hope or dark despair, the *Our Father* remains our
judge and standard. Hence always it must be guarded in the
heart, kept there in trust to illuminate our journey of prayer.

All our prayers must be touched and embraced by the *Our
Father*. The more we come to know this prayer, to really
understand it and enter into it, the more it will form our whole
life of prayer. The *Our Father* then can illuminate all our prayer
with the light of true, properly Christian desire. In this light,
we can more surely pray with confidence, guarded from self-

centeredness and idolatries. When we can pray with real confidence, that our prayer is in the will of God, then we can remember in confidence the words of our Lord, "Truly, truly, I say to you, if you ask anything of the Father, he will give it to you in my name. Hitherto you have asked nothing in my name; ask, and you will receive, that your joy may be full." (Jn 16: 23-24)

The Formative Prayer

The *Our Father* is a formative prayer. When Jesus told us, "Pray then like this ...," He shows us that this prayer has value to God, from "His side", so to speak, in the communion that is prayer. Because of this, the prayer is rightly normative for all our prayer, forming our prayer rightly from "His side." The prayer is also formative from "our side." This prayer calls down the saving work of Christ upon us, forming us according to the holy intention of God. The work of God in Jesus Christ is our salvation, and this work - His saving liturgy - is expressed in the prayer.

Prayer itself continues the work of Christ in the Christian; it is part of our self-gift, our cooperation with Him. For this reason good prayer forms us in Him, and He in us. Formation itself is His work, with the Holy Spirit, gathering us into communion in the Holy Trinity. Good prayer is an affirmation of self-offering, a "yes" to God with Mary. Like soft clay on the potter's wheel, the Christian offers himself to the loving and forming hands of the master potter.

In this prayer we are formed into the mind and heart, so to speak, of God. We are formed into His intention for us from the beginning. Formation has both "negative" and "positive" aspects, seen from a certain point of view. In truth there is only the positive, of course, but formation brings also reformation or change - and change can seem "negative". In this prayer we call ourselves to change, to renewal, to repentance and reform.

We become formed through the power of this prayer that has words given to us by God. By the power of His words God spoke all creation into being. He formed man out of the clay of the ground with His own hands, so to speak. (Gen. 2:7). This prayer is a work of reformation: God reforms us in a return to Him through His internal work - an interior liturgy - of seven stations defined by the seven petitions of the prayer. The formation in us as we pray the prayer, accomplished in the seven petitions of the prayer, has three major components: first a reformation, then a more interior and complete transformation, finally a most complete conformation.

Our reformation occurs through the first part of the interior liturgy, which corresponds to the Liturgy of the Word. Next, at the consecration at the altar, we offer ourselves to transformation in Christ. Finally, in Holy Communion, we are invited into conformation to His life in the Holy Trinity.

The developing formation begins within, in the interior of the soul. It then expresses its truth exteriorly, in the life and works of the person. The fundamental unity of the person must be guarded! There are some theologies that teach "faith alone", with works having no place in the communion of a person with Christ. This is clearly against the wholeness of the person, and the integrity of truth itself: truth is not only an interior reality; it must be expressed, lived. The formation of the person, the disciple, proceeds in these three stages with each having its own interior and exterior expression.

1. Reform through the Word

The beginning stage of formation in the interior liturgy, its first movement and work, is a liturgy of the Word. The predominate work in this first movement is a reformation, a work of reform. This is because the person in the beginning is seeking to respond to Christ now, after some period of struggling without Him. The newly converted wants to reform his life because his life has been exposed by the light of the Word as bankrupt, dark, empty. Occurring in the beginning of discipleship, this time for reform and conversion lasts for some period of time; for some it will last longer than for others.

This period of conversion and reform is the initial movement in the interior liturgy. This is the liturgy of the Word, as here the Word continues to expose, to instruct for conversion, to judge the ways of the world and to teach the ways of God in Christ. The predominate work of Christ in this movement is reform within the soul, and this reform requires the active assent and cooperation of the disciple. This work is truly a work of collaboration: two labor together, Christ and the Christian, while for the Christian it all begins by and continues through His enabling grace.

The new disciple must personally reject the old ways, the ways of the world, the ways of sin. He must turn away from sin and seek out the ways of grace and faith, keeping close to the sacraments and the means of needed grace. This is the time of the reformation of life, for the disciple. How long is the soul to remain in this movement of the liturgy? How much time is needed to complete this part of the work? The answer is hidden in the mind of God, a mystery of grace and human response.

This movement of reform, the interior Liturgy of the Word, is prayed in the petitions,

1.   Deliver us from evil;

2.   Lead us not into temptation;

3.   Forgive us our trespasses as we forgive those who trespass against us.

Exteriorly, the works of conversion and reform must fol-

low: this demands of the disciple a new life of obedience to
Christ, a following of Him in the daytime and at night, in public and in private, in matters of faith and of morals, of the
sacraments and of prayer.

2. The transforming consecration

In the second stage of formation, the Liturgy of
Consecration, the predominate work is a transformation - the
transformation into Christ. This interior work corresponds to
the consecration at the altar in our Liturgy of the Mass, when
humble bread and wine are transformed into the Body, Blood,
Soul and Divinity of the Lord Jesus Christ. In the interior
Liturgy of Consecration, the person is brought to the altar
within his own soul and by grace offers himself in union with
Christ. Here the person becomes a heart-priest, offering himself body and blood, soul and humanity, to be united with
Christ in His complete Self-gift for the Church and for all
humanity.

Consecration brings a new power to our vocation, revealing new meaning of our priesthood in Christ. Indeed the meaning of our life is now illuminated freshly in the dawn of a new
and previously unknown day. The sacred passion of Christ
becomes strangely beautiful, at the altar of consecration.
Suffering, the cross, sacrifice - and most crucially love - are
seen differently now in the light of transforming Resurrection
glory.

Transforming consecration uncovers the very identity of
the Christian. The mystery of who I am, and why I am here,
and why did God make me, all become more clear in the illumination of His Self-gift, and in the union of my own self-offering with His. There, at the sacred altar of His cross and my
own, there at the center of the church and of religion, the
meaning of my life is unveiled. There, at the precious work on

earth of His eternal priesthood, my own priesthood becomes defined and directed.

This movement of transformation, the Consecration at the Altar, is prayed in the petitions,

4.   Give us this day our daily bread

5.   Thy will be done on earth as it is in heaven.

Transformation in Christ is predominately His work, the work of His saving liturgy. Our part is to respond, to accept, to cooperate and to yield to the power of His life and His will.

3. Communion: the conforming union

In the final stage of formation, in the interior Liturgy of Holy Communion, the predominate work is a conformation – the conforming of the person to His life in all ways. It is here, in the holy of holies, in most intimate communion in Christ, where human lives radiate with the splendor of the Spirit and the kenosis of the Son. Here the soul rests in the Holy Trinity, and the Holy Trinity in the soul. Here the invitation of the Lord, "Remain in Me," is embraced as His remaining is experienced.

In this movement of the interior liturgy, the person celebrates the Holy Trinity with his life. In and through the Son, in the unity of the Holy Spirit, the soul beholds the glory of the Father and seeks only to enact that beatitude with the humble worship of his humanity. Whether the faithful "yes" leads to years of ministry in His name, or whether it leads to quick martyrdom, God is trusted and loved. The soul is the lowly handmaiden of the Lord, who magnifies His holy name: blessed be the name of the Lord!

In conformity to Christ, the soul is for Him, and in Him for the Church. The soul is His, and all she is, is for Him. In Him the soul is given to the Church, as John was given to Mary at the foot of the cross. And as Mary was given to John, so the Church becomes the beloved of the soul in this communion of the interior liturgy. As Christ was wholly given for the Church, to empty Himself for her, so also the Christian is here formed to that self-emptying, out of love for His Bride and Spouse.

It is martyrdom, whether a living martyrdom or a bloody one, that radiates the glory of the Holy Trinity. It is conformity to the kenosis of Christ that continues His glorification among men. This is the worship of His saints; this is the cross embraced; this is the radiance of the burning bush made more glorious by the free assent of a human person.

This movement of conformation, the Holy Communion of the interior liturgy, is prayed in the petitions,

6.   Thy kingdom come,

7.   Hallowed be thy name.

Conforming union with Christ is celebrated within, in this interior liturgy of contemplative prayer; it is celebrated exteriorly in a human life in imitation of Christ and the saints. This is life in the Holy Spirit, this is the witness of Pentecost, these are lives of heroic virtue and Christian splendor.

Prayer of the Heart-Priest

The ordained priest is like an image or symbol of the Christian life itself - or perhaps more an icon, than an image. The ordained priest offers sacrifice to God, as we are all called to offer our own bodies a living sacrifice (Rom 12:1). The ordained priest intercedes for the Church, as we are all called to pray for others in authentic charity. The ordained priest proclaims the Word of God, as we all are called to do. The ordained priest stands, on behalf of the Church, *in persona Christi capitas* - in the person of Christ the head - and in this role the ordained priest is unique. Yet even so we all, as members of His body, are called to represent Christ among men.

The priest also, in his role of mediation, reveals to us something essential to love: its giving and its receiving. The priest receives from the people in order to offer to God, and he receives from God in order to offer to the people. Worship is dialogue, prayer is dialogue and love is dialogue. Love calls forth exchange between persons, always giving and receiving. The priest facilitates this exchange, enabling us, as the interior liturgy proceeds, to grow toward the perfection of love.

An icon, in the Eastern tradition, holds a quality of transparency to the heavens, and to the eternal realities abiding beyond the veils of this creation. Each particular icon directs the prayerful heart to particular and beautiful realities in the heavenly places. An icon is not a symbol of those realities, but a window to them through which the contemplative eyes of the heart can gaze. The ordained priest is an icon for us, the icon of Christ upon the cross, through which we see into the eternal priesthood of the Son: the one high priest who eternally stands to make intercession for us. (Heb 7:25) Every priest is this icon, given to the Church and for the Church by virtue of ordination. The holy priests who glow with the unction of love and grace, as well as those not so wholly given to His will, all nevertheless represent Christ and direct the Church toward Christ. They represent Him for us, and intercede to God in Christ on our behalf. And they represent to us all, in their ordained priesthood, the crucial reality of our own priesthood of the heart.

Every Christian is called to a priesthood of the heart: to discover in Christ the riches of His life in the Holy Trinity, and to enter the mystery of our being in the image of God. The priesthood of the heart is not a vocation among vocations; it is essential to the human heart. Unlike the ordained priest who is called out from the people to be priest for them, the heart-priest remains common to the people, doing his part by example and by ministry to enable the common priesthood of all.

The *Our Father* is a priestly prayer: a prayer of intercession for others. Moses shows us a great example of the heart-priest, the man willing to "stand in the breach" between God and His people (Ps 106:23) pleading in intercession for them. The continuing conversation between Moses and God unveils many mysteries of prayer for us, but most especially this quality of mercy in the heart of the heart-priest: Moses pleaded again and again for God's mercy for the people, who hardly seemed to know their right hand from their left. Yet they were the people God had chosen, and would use for His glory.

The *Our Father* forms us into heart-priests, praying in intercession for His people. In Christ, into whom we are in truth gathered by faith and Baptism, we pray always in union with Him - in His name - and so join in His unique and perfect mediation. (1 Tim 2:5) In this prayer we are formed into His intercession: we become His priests. Whether in the priesthood of the laity which all share by Baptism, or in the additional and particular ministry of the ordained priests, this prayer forms our intercession with Christ for His people.

The first word in our English translation, "Our", immediately places us in priestly intercession. We cannot repeat the prayer in separation or isolation - if we are faithful to the words Jesus gave us, we must pray in communion, and for others. We pray for our daily bread, for our forgiveness, for our freedom through temptations, for our deliverance from evil. The words themselves place us in intercession, in prayer for others, in prayer on behalf of all. The words form us into a priesthood of the heart, in Christ.

The experience of Moses reveals an essential reality for

intercessory prayer, seen in the theophany at the burning bush. (Ex. 3:2) Although the bush was burning, it was not consumed. In all human experience, when fire ignites some material, the material gives itself to the flame and is consumed: the gift leads to destruction. Yet in the burning bush shown to Moses, the bush gave itself fully to the flame, yet the flame did not destroy it! There was in this self-giving, this being for the fire that disclosed the great mystery: the bush was safe even through the fire. In this revelation of God, in this unveiling of His name to Moses, Moses was allowed to see into the mystery of God's interior life and being. God gives, but is not consumed. God is being itself: God is His own being and life and love-gift: I AM WHO I AM.

This revelation of God's love as Gift is disclosed most perfectly in Christ: His gift of self extended even to His death, yet a death that was not unto destruction. Jesus burned with the light and love of God, yet like the burning bush was not consumed. This is the promise to Moses, and more clearly to us: we too are called into a life for the other; we will not be consumed. We find life in self-gift. In the giving of ourselves - even if unto death - we will not be consumed. This is the overwhelming power of faith in the resurrection.

The *Our Father* calls us into the priesthood of the heart, a life-long liturgy of intercession for others, a life of self-gift. The interior liturgy itself, flowing from the last petition toward the first, begins with obvious prayer of intercession (deliver us, lead us not into temptation, forgive us, give us). The liturgy then proceeds toward the more interior intercession of the cross, Self-sacrifice itself, from which our bread from heaven comes. At the altar of the cross, at the source of our daily bread, our own priestly intercession is confirmed. From here unfolds the mystical dimensions of the prayer, and our own priesthood. From the cross is the will revealed: that will that we pray to be done on earth as in heaven, the will that defines our priesthood. From the cross, in the light of His will, is revealed the glory of the kingdom for which we plead, for which we labor as priests. From the cross, His will revealed, His kingdom sought above all, is then unveiled the holiness of His name above all names, the name that illuminates our priesthood with the glory of God.

The Prayer of Spiritual Direction

The *Our Father* traces a journey: an interior journey from the darkness of the lost, into personal relationship with Him in His light and life. The prayer is of seven petitions, tracing seven stages or steps of discipleship - the stages of the inner pilgrimage of the soul.

Because the seven petitions trace the seven stages of discipleship, they give us the guideposts of the whole journey. The seven petitions serve as markers, describing briefly, yet very helpfully, the sequence of stations that lead us step by step from the beginning to the end of our journey with Christ. Because these markers are given to us by the Lord Himself, they serve as the norm and the standard of all spiritual direction. The seven petitions, with the seven interior movements of the saving work of Christ that they call forth, give guidance to all religious guides and direction to all spiritual directors. When we pray this prayer, we are asking for and we are receiving the spiritual direction of the Lord Himself.

The seven stations of the interior liturgy, corresponding to the seven petitions of the *Our Father*, stand within the three major movements of the liturgy of Christ: first, His liturgy of the Word, worked in His earthly ministry up to His passion; second, the consecration at the altar of His cross and the ministry after His resurrection; third, the communion enabled through the gift of the Holy Spirit after Pentecost, and the continuing ministry of Christ through His Church until the end of the age. These three major movements of the saving work of Christ continue to be re-presented in the Church in her most holy liturgy of the Eucharist, the Mass: first the liturgy of the Word, second the consecration at the altar, and finally the holy communion.

Because these three powerful movements of saving and divine work act within the soul of human persons, we are not surprised to find that the soul responds to these movements of God's work with movements of spiritual growth. God works within us, and we grow. His saving liturgy unfolds in three movements, we respond through three stages of spiritual growth. That is, the traditional three stages of the spiritual life - beginner, proficient, perfect - are our human responses to the three movements of the saving liturgy of Christ. The traditional three stages of the interior life of the soul - also called the purgative, the illuminative, and the unitive stages - are our human responses to the three great movements of the work of Christ: the liturgy of the Word, the consecration at the altar of the cross, and the holy communion. These stand as the great and major markers of the Christian vocation. These are the great lights along the pilgrimage of the soul, our spiritual direction.

Spiritual direction is a gift to the Church, a ministry enabled in Christ. The Holy Spirit is the spiritual director of the soul, Who teaches and guides and recalls to the soul the truth given us by Christ. The Spirit follows the pattern of the Son, directing human persons through three spiritual stages in their journey into life in Christ. As Jesus worked His saving work in the first disciples in three stages, so also the Spirit today leads and directs us through three stages in our Christian life. As the liturgy of the Mass re-presents the saving work of

Christ in three movements, so also does the Spirit direct us in the interior liturgy in three major movements - all of these liturgies corresponding to one another. The Spirit first directs us in the liturgy of the Word, which corresponds to the purgative stage of the beginner. The Spirit next directs us in the consecration at the altar, which corresponds to the illuminative stage of the proficient. The Spirit finally directs us in the communion of life in the Holy Trinity, which corresponds to the unitive stage of the perfect.

In the interior liturgy, then, the Spirit directs us through the seven stations of the saving work of Christ, within the three major movements of His great work of redemption:

First the movement of purgation, the liturgy of the Word, prayed in the stations,

1. Deliver us from evil;

2. Lead us not into temptation;

3. Forgive us our trespasses as we forgive those who trespass against us.

Next the great movement of illumination, the consecration at the altar to a priesthood of the heart, prayed in the stations,

4. Give us this day our daily bread;

5. Thy will be done on earth as it is in heaven.

Finally, the culminating movement of perfection, the divine communion prayed in the stations,

6. Thy kingdom come;

7. Hallowed be thy name.

As the prayer of spiritual direction, then, the *Our Father* sets within us the guideposts of the interior liturgy of Christ. The Spirit directs us, first, following the first conversion from sin to Christ, in the crucial struggle against evil that must be the urgent concern of the soul in the beginning stage of the spiritual journey. The *Our Father* directs us, in this time of confrontation and decision, in the personal contest against evil, against temptations, and against that interior hardness that would close our own hearts against the mercy of God.

If the soul continues to follow Christ in sincerity and generosity, the liturgy continues. The next major movement of His saving work brings the soul to stand before the altar, and to hear the vocation to the priesthood of the heart: consecration. The *Our Father* directs us, in this time of illumination and sanctification, to the table at that altar, the table of the bread from heaven. It is here that the Spirit illuminates the icon that is the cross, to reveal the mission of the Son in the eternal will of the Father in heaven.

The third and ultimate movement of the Spirit in the interior liturgy of human persons occurs in correspondence with that great ignition of lives of holiness in the Church following the epiphany of Pentecost. The *Our Father* directs us, in this time of communion and active contemplation, to a personal human enactment of sanctity. This is the perfection of human life, made in the image of God. This is our vocation from the beginning. This is our end, as human persons. This is the living of our consecration, our priesthood, our part in the kingdom here on earth which is the Church. Here, we express in human ways and in human beauty, the holy name of God our creator and our Father.

The seven stations of the interior liturgy are made understandable and clear by the seven petitions of the *Our Father* which describe them. The meaning of each petition illuminates its particular station. It is also helpful, for further study and prayer, to pray this with the holy Saint Teresa of Jesus (of Avila). Her insight into the human soul, as like a beautiful castle of many rooms, can be compared with these stations of the interior liturgy, seen through the *Our Father*.[30]

The Prayer of Examination of Conscience

As a prayer of light upon one's struggling and growing conscience, the *Our Father* is best prayed audibly yet while alone. As one person professing out loud these words from God in His presence only, each of us speaks as a prophet and listens as a disciple. We each speak and hear the call of Christ to be oneself truly, fully, really. This prayer recalls each of us to himself - or rather, to his authentic and true self - with the simplicity and the power of divine truth. The prayer is a door and a series of doors into deeper and deeper, fuller and more complete communion with Him in the Holy Trinity.

The call of the *Our Father* - a call we are to hear most personally as vocation - is dynamic, having a movement and a direction both out of the darkness of sin and into the brilliant and fruitful light of life. How we hunger for this light, this life! Through each petition, through each movement with Him in our life in Him, the words of this prayer scrutinize and examine the heart. Because this prayer directs the heart step by step toward the Father who awaits us, it also questions us: "Here is God's word to you; what is your answer?" The intention and desire of God probe the human heart. In this way, the prayer tests and explores our conscience, our sincerity, our authenticity, our answer.

Our own willingness must be wed to His intention, as we pray in examination of conscience! The refining fire is of no use, if it only separates for a moment and does nothing to burn out the impurity. The *Our Father* brings light to the wounded and the confused, directing and leading a human person out of the hostile dead-dry desert, toward the fertile oasis that is indeed paradise. The human person must want to follow! Each of us, in praying this prayer, must also participate in His liturgy interiorly - personally and generously. The Church teaches us that we are to offer "full, conscious, and active participation" in the holy liturgy of the Mass.[31] Our need is to give this full "yes" to God's call and God's work - a "yes" not merely vocal, but fully human. This need for full participation in His work extends as well into the work within, the interior liturgy.

The *Our Father*, as examination of conscience, asks our obedience layer by layer, step by step, and station by station in the interior liturgy, petition by petition in the prayer. As the prayer of formation, each forming work is as well an invitation requiring our "yes". As the prayer of heart-priesthood, each rite of sacrifice requires as well our part, our donation. As the normative prayer and judge of all our life of prayer, each individual petition measures the desire and willingness of the heart. The *Our Father* in this way questions as it illuminates; the divine fire it enkindles within the human heart is meant to purge and purify, as it forms within that heart the new life in Jesus Christ.

If we are to benefit from this particular dimension of the prayer, we must want to know the truth about ourselves. This requires a certain courage of us, or fortitude, because the truth will demand change and change may seem very difficult. Humility also is needed, because without humility one cannot bear to know the truth about oneself. The truth seems to be death to a proud man, yet it is life to the humble. The *Our Father* brings light within the soul and reveals the person to himself unto life, if he can receive it with fortitude and humility.

Petition by petition, the prayer examines the conscience and asks for the truth of the person who is praying. When I pray, "deliver us from evil," the questions come: Do I need deliverance from evil? Do I really want freedom from evil, and the sins I still desire? Am I willing to turn to this sin or that sin never again? Do I really believe that "evil" is indeed horrible, and is death to me?

Do I really mean "us" when I pray this prayer? Am I concerned for the deliverance of all persons - my friends, my family, my enemies, the strangers, the poor and ignorant and defenseless as well as the rich and powerful? I am asking for deliverance for every human person - am I willing to do my necessary part to help in this petition? Am I personally willing to do what I can to free all from bondage to evils?

In this way each petition of the prayer turns to question each of us as we pray. If I sincerely ask God to bring some truth to exist, then I place myself under obligation as well to that truth. If I ask God to do something, then I must be willing to do my part to cooperate with His doing. God indeed works through His Church. The Church is the Body of Christ, remaining on this earth until He comes again in glory, sent to finish His great work, sent to be His sacrament of salvation, sent in His name. In the sense that I am called to be a member of this Church, I am Church. In asking God of any good thing, I implicitly am offering myself as His instrument, His minister, His means to that end. The *Our Father*, the most perfect of prayers and the norm of all prayer, therefore most perfectly also probes each human conscience and seeks a beautiful "yes" to God.

The Prayer of Liturgy and Sacrament

There is yet one more sense in which we say that the *Our Father* is the prayer of the interior liturgy. In the seven stations of the interior liturgy, through which we pray the seven petitions of the *Our Father*, we also pray to receive from God the particular graces appropriate to the seven sacraments of the

Church. It is through the liturgy - that is, through the saving work of Jesus Christ, that we receive the sacraments of the Church. The *Our Father* leads us into an inner, spiritual and personal sacramental union with Christ. This prayer, of course, does not in any way replace the communal liturgy, or the holy sacraments of the Church! Rather, alongside the communal liturgy, the interior liturgy prays for and makes place for personal graces which correspond to the graces of the seven sacraments of the Church.

The liturgy is a work, indeed His saving work. Liturgy cannot be separated from sacrament, for we also affirm truly, "The saving work of his holy and sanctifying humanity is the sacrament of salvation, which is revealed and active in the Church's sacraments."[32] That is, the liturgy of the Church brings forth the sacrament of Christ Himself, through the seven sacraments that are celebrated and communicated through the liturgies. Liturgy and sacrament are intimately, necessarily and interdependently celebrated in the worship and life of the people of God.

So also does the interior liturgy, celebrated in the inner life of the disciple of Christ, call forth sacramental graces from His saving work. The interior liturgy calls forth the seven sacramental graces in intentional and specific ways - called forth as they are needed in the journey of the soul, in the growth made manifest in the stages of the interior life.

The sequence and flow of graces called forth in the interior liturgy are as follows:

First the graces of the first conversion, called forth in the liturgy of the Word, are prayed for in the first three stations.

1. "Deliver us from evil." Here the sacramental grace of Baptism is called forth in the work of Christ.

2. "Lead us not into temptation." Here the sacramental grace

of Confirmation is called forth.

3. "Forgive us our trespasses as we forgive those who trespass against us." Here the sacramental grace of Reconciliation is called forth.

Next the graces of illumination, the graces of consecration to a priesthood of the heart, are prayed for in the next two stations at the altar.

4. "Give us this day our daily bread." Here the sacramental grace of Holy Eucharist is called forth.

5. "Thy will be done on earth as it is in heaven." Here the sacramental grace of Anointing is called forth.

Finally, the graces of the sacraments of communion, the crowning work of perfection, are prayed for in the last two stations.

6. "Thy kingdom come." Here the sacramental grace of Orders is called forth in the work of Christ.

7. "Hallowed be thy name." Here the sacramental grace of Marriage is called forth.

These sacramental graces will be explored and discussed in more detail as we listen intently to the petitions, one by one, of the prayer. For now, however, it may be helpful to reflect upon the flow of these sacramental graces as a whole - the stream of grace in the union of all the seven sacraments - as they flow one by one from the pierced side of Christ, from His saving work of love. They flow to us one by one out of His liturgy on the cross into our souls to give life, to bathe the human soul in the healing, saving, resurrecting power of the life of God.

First flows the grace of Baptism, delivering us from evil. This is the new birth absolutely necessary to enter the kingdom of God, the beginning of the interior liturgy: "the basis of the whole Christian life, the gateway to life in the Spirit, and the door which gives access to the other sacraments."[33] Next flows the grace of Confirmation, "the completion of baptismal grace"[34] that specifically enables the strength needed for the struggles that must come to us in Christ. Just as the actual Sacrament of Confirmation strengthens the Christian to stand against trial to be His witness in the world, so the interior graces flowing in the interior liturgy in the second station give the grace needed to stand against the interior struggles against temptation: "lead us not into temptation."

In the third station of the interior liturgy, if he has indeed progressed to this stage, the soul has the crucial need and privilege of final, immediate preparation for the altar. This is the close of the ascetical stage of Christian life and prayer, and the very door to the mystical life, final preparation for the truly interior life, the life of the contemplative, the prayer of infused contemplation. Here the graces of blessed Reconciliation are essential, and are called forth in the petition for the forgiveness of our sin - linked in mystery to the necessary forgiveness on our part to those who have trespassed against us. Just as the Sacraments of Baptism and Confirmation open access to - and Reconciliation immediately prepares the Christian for - Holy Eucharist, so also in the interior liturgy the three petitions "deliver us from evil," "lead us not into temptation," and "forgive us our trespasses as we forgive those who have trespassed against us" prepare us for the altar. These petitions call forth the graces identified with those three sacraments of the Church, to prepare us for the interior consecration at the altar, and the petition "give us this day our daily bread."

The fourth station of the interior liturgy begins wholly new insight and understanding, with entry into the illuminative stage of the soul. Mysteries not understood in the liturgy of the Word now receive light, illuminated in new graces. This is now the second major movement of the Spirit, accomplishing the saving work of Christ in the soul. In the fourth station of the interior liturgy we are called to the altar within, the altar of consecration to heart-priesthood: to a life of self-offering and intercession. We pray, standing with Christ at His altar, at the foot of His cross with Mary and His beloved disciple, and we say, "Give us this day our daily bread." Here we open our own hearts to His sacred food that the world knows not - the food of obedience. The Bread received in the fourth station then empowers the work of obedience in the fifth. In the fifth station we can say with Jesus, "I have food to eat of which you do not know. ... My food is to do the will of him who sent me, and to accomplish his work." (Jn 4: 32-34) In the fourth station, the graces of Eucharist flow forth to us who ask - the graces of the food from heaven. In the fifth, these graces begin to reveal their fruits.

The fifth station of the interior liturgy continues at the altar of the cross, now gazing through the icon of the Passion into the mysteries within the suffering of the Son. Praying for the will of God on earth - even within oneself - "as it is in heaven," we call to God for the graces of His anointing upon our own self-offering. Gazing upon the suffering Servant Christ, peering into the mysterious will of the Father who sent Him, we pray for the graces needed in our particular part in His saving passion. The Sacrament of the Anointing enables:

> Union with the passion of Christ. By the grace of this sacrament the sick person receives the strength and the gift of uniting himself more closely to Christ's Passion: in a certain way he is consecrated to bear fruit by configuration to the Savior's redemptive Passion. Suffering, a consequence of original sin, acquires a new meaning; it becomes a participation in the saving work of Jesus.[35]

Grace corresponding to this unique sacrament is called forth as we pray at this station for our participation in His holy will. As the Father sent the Son, so the Son sends the Church, sends us, sends you and me.

The sixth and seventh stations of the interior liturgy take

us to the final movement of the Spirit in the soul, the last movement interiorly of the saving work of Christ: the unitive stage of the perfect. These last stations call forth, in their petitions of the *Our Father*, the graces of the sacraments that are called "the sacraments at the service of communion"[36]: Orders and Matrimony. These are the sacraments "directed toward the salvation of others."[37] These are the stations ordered to our final fruitfulness in the apostolate of the Church, our end from the beginning.

These interior stations comprise the last major movement of the interior liturgy. This final work of the Spirit within corresponds, in our communal liturgy of holy Mass, to the concluding rite of Holy Communion. As the Holy Communion is to empower us to live Christ in the world, so too these final two stations of the interior liturgy call forth the grace to serve in Him and to fulfill our vocation.

Of the last two sacraments, Holy Orders and Matrimony, those "at the service of communion," which one is ordered to the response of God to the petition "Thy kingdom come," and which to the petition "Hallowed be thy name"? Certainly Holy Orders is recognized in the Church as the sacrament that is to configure the man to Christ the Head, to serve the Church His Bride *in persona Christi Capitas*.[38] From the perspective of the person called, the complete and perfect among vocations is that one in closest imitation of the life and Person of Christ the Lord. In this sense, the priesthood objectively offers the higher vocation, higher than the married state. Of course, whether a man attains a higher sanctity in his lifetime through his life as a priest, than he would have as a faithful member of the laity, possibly married - this cannot be known or predicted.

Interiorly, however, in the interior liturgy of Christ in the soul, the final work of Christ is not ordered to the preparation for union, but to the union itself. Marriage in Christ reveals to some extent, both to the couple and through the couple to the world, the eschatological union with Him that is seen here and now by analogy in Christian marriage. In Orders, the man can find most perfect configuration to Christ Himself. In Matrimony, the couple can find, through the graces of their marriage, configuration to the final purpose of Christ: His work, His liturgy, is ordered to spousal union with Him. By means of His service, the Bride is made ready. Through His ministry, the wedding feast of the Lamb is enabled. Thus in the liturgy, the sixth station prepares for the seventh: "Thy kingdom come," which calls for the graces of priesthood, prepares for and enables the union in the holy name, our spiritual marriage. Matrimony stands in the dignity of highest icon of the human vocation to union with God in Christ. This is what Christ came to establish, this is the mission of the ordained priesthood, this is the purpose of human life itself: union with God in Jesus Christ the Son.

In the sixth station then, as we pray, "thy kingdom come," we pray immediately for the Church: the Church is the kingdom begun on earth. In our prayer, we call forth the enabling grace of the sacrament of Orders poured forth from the side of Christ to gather and build up His people. In the seventh station, praying that the holy name be hallowed, we stand with Him awaiting the great feast: the wedding of the Lamb and His Church. In marriage, the bride is given participation in the name of the groom! In marriage, community in the one name is received: the two become one, the bride truly becomes one flesh with her spouse. So too in the interior liturgy, at this place of culmination of the saving work of Christ, the soul stands with her Spouse, she receives His holy name, and the mystical and spiritual marriage is accomplished. "Hallowed be thy name," is the prayer of the final station of the interior liturgy, which calls forth the grace of Matrimony from the outpoured powers of Christ our Lord.

Matrimony holds a most exalted place in the interior liturgy! Matrimony is the sacrament first established by God in the Garden of Eden, before there was any sin in mankind. He gave this sacred covenant with its grace, its vocation, its dignity. Matrimony is the sacrament of communion of persons, communion such that the two become one, communion through covenant founded upon love.

All sacraments resemble icons, which they transcend by their unique power to communicate Christ. They resemble icons in that sacraments are windows into the mysteries of the heavens, revealing in their outward appearance something of their inner spiritual reality. This sacrament - Matrimony - begins to penetrate the most mysterious of spiritual realities, the Holy Trinity. "The mystery of the Most Holy Trinity is the central mystery of Christian faith and life. It is the mystery of God in himself."[39]

Matrimony directs the Christian - indeed it is intended to direct the whole world - to the ultimate mystery of the inner life of the triune God: three divine Persons who are one God. The tender dialogue of husband and wife, expressed in all the human exchange and mutual response of their masculinity and femininity, radiates with a certain glory having origin in the Holy Trinity. The giving and receiving of love, which in spite of our brokenness gives such delight and joy in the human covenant of marriage, prepares ours hearts and minds for a giving and receiving and a joy unbounded by sin. In Jesus we hear the staggering dimensions of the love that is our destiny and vocation: He, the Son, ever receiving all from the Father, willingly empties Himself for love.

In the petition, "hallowed be thy name," we are directed into this great mystery of the name of God. The baptismal formula emphasizes this mystery: we are baptized into the <u>name</u> - not the (plural) <u>names</u>- of the Father and of the Son and of the

Holy Spirit. God has one name, not three. There are three Persons, yet one name. This is the same mystery, analogously in human expression, found in the sacrament of Matrimony in which the inner reality of love is expressed in the two who become one.

This great petition for the holy name, which recalls the great and holy sacrament of Matrimony by analogy, stands as first in the seven petitions in the *Our Father*. The depths and ultimate nature of this petition are suggested in the *Catechism*, which states, "This petition embodies all the others."[40] The grace of the communion of persons is hidden in this petition, "hallowed be thy name." The communion of persons, united in the communion in Christ with God, is our ultimate vocation and destiny. To this destiny all our steps are ordered, directed in simplicity and truth through the seven petitions of the *Our Father*, calling forth grace as we need it, grace revealed in the seven facets of Christ, the seven sacraments.

PART II - PRAYING HIS LIFE; LIVING HIS PRAYER

The prayer *Our Father* is very brief and very simple. The fullness of truth that this prayer holds within its simplicity and brevity is revealed to us only in time, as we pray with patience and reverence. The rich treasure of this prayer, the profound value it holds, is not given up to anyone content merely to recite it mechanically. The gift of this prayer is like the gift of a living thing: it grows, develops, unfolds, bears fruit in due season to one who will work with it. The prayer is like the seed planted by the farmer, revealing its inner potential only in the proper seasons of its growth. Remaining rich with mystery even to the farmer, the seed unfolds its meaning first as a blade coming out of the ground, then the ear, and finally the full grain in the ear. (i.e. Mk 4:26-29) So too the *Our Father* unfolds for us in three stages, three major movements of the Holy Spirit in the interior work of Christ in the soul. The *Our Father* unfolds within the soul as it is prayed again and again, in growing devotion and fidelity, as it is treasured in the soul and watered by grace. The *Our Father* unveils its meaning with its beauty as the soul itself grows and matures under the guidance of the Spirit sent to continue the work of Christ. The liturgy is illustrated in figure 2 (page 84).

The interior liturgy unfolds in three major movements, seen in the Church as the three stages of the spiritual life along the road of discipleship, the path to holiness. These three major movements include seven stations, or resting places of prayer and reflection, where particular works of Christ are completed. Each of these seven stations has its prayer, its own meditation, characterized by one of the seven petitions of the *Our Father*.

As the work of Christ proceeds in the soul, the interior liturgy unfolds through its seven stations and its three movements. As the liturgy unfolds, the prayer deepens - union with Christ deepens, becoming more authentic and personal and

Figure 2: The Three movements of the Interior Liturgy
(This chart is to be read from the bottom, up.)
In the interior liturgy, grace descends and the Christian ascends toward God, his vocation, through the three movements of the liturgy. These movements correspond to the traditional three stages of Catholic spiritual theology.

Our Father, who art in heaven...

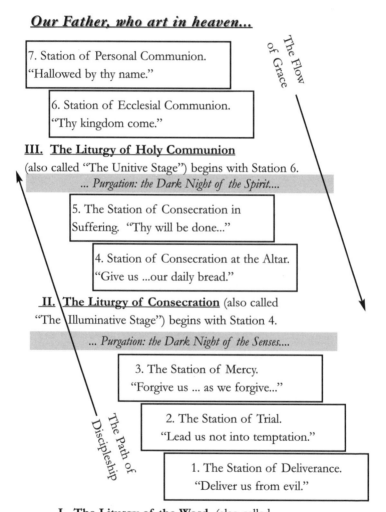

7. Station of Personal Communion.
"Hallowed by thy name."

6. Station of Ecclesial Communion.
"Thy kingdom come."

III. The Liturgy of Holy Communion
(also called "The Unitive Stage") begins with Station 6.
... Purgation: the Dark Night of the Spirit....

5. The Station of Consecration in Suffering. "Thy will be done..."

4. Station of Consecration at the Altar.
"Give us ...our daily bread."

 II. The Liturgy of Consecration (also called "The Illuminative Stage") begins with Station 4.

... Purgation: the Dark Night of the Senses....

3. The Station of Mercy.
"Forgive us ... as we forgive..."

2. The Station of Trial.
"Lead us not into temptation."

1. The Station of Deliverance.
"Deliver us from evil."

I. The Liturgy of the Word (also called "The Purgative Stage.") begins with Station 1.

complete. The words of the *Our Father* are so familiar! So
many times have we repeated this formula! Yet as the interior
liturgy proceeds in the soul, working as it were through the
path of this prayer, the prayer brings forth its purpose.

Our Father, who art in heaven....

Standing in prayer before the Father in Jesus Christ the
Son, facing His awesome and infinite glory, bathed in the eternal blazing love of the Holy Spirit, we pronounce this truth of
our vocation and our destiny. We dare to say in Christ, "Our
Father." The *Catechism* uses and stresses this word "dare",
describing our inner response to such a salutation to God.[41]
How can we dare to call God "Father"? We hardly know how
to begin to understand God in Himself, in the Holy Trinity of
Father, Son and Holy Spirit, three Persons in One God. We do
not understand the relation of God the Father with God the
Son - how can we possibly understand our own "sonship",
whether as sons or daughters, in Christ?

To begin this prayer is to enter mystery! Jesus said, "...no
one knows the Son except the Father, and no one knows the
Father except the Son and any one to whom the Son chooses
to reveal him." (Mt 11: 27) We can never understand the Father
except in Christ the Son. We can never understand our prayer
of His own words, "Our Father, who art in heaven," unless He
reveals to us in Himself the divine Being, love and life of Father
and Son. We do dare, because He calls us. We dare, because He
promises.

Our hunger and our thirst seek to find this place within
the divine Being, the Holy Trinity. Our very being makes sense
only in Him: in Him is the meaning of the great mystery of the
human person. In Him, uttering this simple truth that radiates
both light and warmth within us, the humbling dignity of our

nature made in the image of God is illuminated. Contained in this phrase, "Our Father who art in heaven," is mysteriously the meaning of every human life on earth. We are made for God, to live in the glory of His life, in loving relationship worthy of persons in Persons.

These first words, forming the salutation of the prayer, are both the beginning and the end of the prayer. These words awaken the beginning of our return to Him, and anticipate the final end in Him. Why did God make you? The old Baltimore *Catechism* answered that God made us to know Him, to love Him, to serve Him in this world and to be happy with Him forever in the next. This ultimate beatitude in communion in the Holy Trinity is contained in this, the beginning of our prayer.

We cannot receive the gift of prayer with God apart from His gift of undeserved and enabling grace. He stirs us to realize our emptiness and hunger. He touches us with His life. He calls us into consecration; He takes us by the hand, and walks with us and in us into the life of charity. Only in the Son can we approach the Father, for no one comes to the Father except through Him. In the Son we begin this prayer, and as we pray, we discover our beginning and our end. Our life is in Christ, and in Him for the Father; apart from Him we have no existence, not being itself, nor life. The journey that is a human life begins in Him, if it begins; it is ever toward Him, if it progresses; and it is finally in Him, if it finds its meaning and reason and true intention.

Section 1. The First Movement:
the Liturgy of the Word

The first movement of the interior liturgy begins with His work in us of conversion and Baptism. With the grace of Baptism, now empowering us to a new life in Christ, we begin our journey of discipleship and our part in the saving work of Christ. This movement corresponds to the stage of the beginners, or the purgative stage of the spiritual life, in traditional Catholic spirituality.

The Concerns of the First Movement

A call to repentance

In this beginning of the spiritual life - the Christian life - we hardly understand what we have actually begun. We are called to love God completely, with our whole heart and mind and soul and strength; we are called to love neighbor as self. We hardly know, in the beginning, how far we are from this call! Yet it is also true that we who have begun the journey in Christ, are now infinitely closer to our destiny in Him than we were before.

The call to repentance is a call at once to turn from evil, and to turn to God. We hear this most clearly in the first petition of this station, "Deliver us from evil." Do we, however, pray this with the understanding and the integrity of heart that the prayer deserves? In the beginning, the answer most certainly is no - yet as we grow in Christ, and as we grow in prayer relationship with Him, so also does the sincerity of these words and the others of this prayer. An honest examination of conscience will usually reveal that we do not hate evil as we should.

The fullness of repentance would call us to love God completely, and to love neighbor as self - and so also to hate evil completely as the antithesis of goodness, and the enemy of God, that it is. We do not hate evil as we should. The bitter results of sin assault our peace and our happiness every day! Evil breaks our hearts, and tears at our lives, every day! Yet we do not hate evil enough; still we cling to it. Because of sin, all of nature is in disharmony: sickness attacks us, the earth's hostility rages against us with hurricanes, with earthquakes, with tornados, with floods and with droughts. Our mothers suffer, die and leave us behind; our fathers weaken in illness, grow feeble before us, and pass on. Our beloved spouses fail, age, and die. Sometimes even our children, so innocent, fall victim to cancer, to birth defect, to agonies and to death. Yet after all this – after all these messengers of the horror of sin and of evil – even still we do not hate evil enough. And because we do not hate evil enough, we do not repent wholeheartedly, and we do not turn to God with wholeness of heart and mind and soul and strength.

This is an often unsteady time, a time of spiritual dangers and temptations. Here, we are only beginning to turn away from the former ways and toward the ways of Christ and His Church. The old ways are still very near in memory, still present in our thoughts by habit. Old friends may not understand that we have begun a new life, and so they come to tempt us to the old pleasures and former values.

We are only beginning to know the teachings of the Church, the sacred revelation that has been passed down, the moral truths of the Christian life, the mysteries of the sacraments, and the blessed life of prayer. These four "pillars of the faith" are crucial to the Christian life! None of these four – doctrine, sacraments, morals, and prayer – can be overlooked or neglected without serious impediment to the liturgy within, and to our life in Christ.

We who are in the first movement, or we who are helping

a brother or sister who is in the first movement, must be careful to preserve a healthy balance of these four pillars. Unfortunately, we can find around us examples of Catholics who have not guarded well the integrity of their faith. Some Catholics, for example, treasure the doctrines of the faith - as well they should - yet neglect some or all of the other crucial components. Some are especially tempted toward the merely mental embrace of the faith: "all head and no heart." Of course this does not do justice to the whole and living truth of Christ.

Other poor witnesses are also around us: Catholics who in some sense devoutly partake of the sacraments, yet fail to hold to the other pillars. They may attend daily Mass, for example, and even regularly receive Reconciliation, yet exteriorly and with little understanding or repentance. Some may frequent the sacraments yet may have scandalous beliefs on contraception or abortion. Some may regularly attend Mass, yet with little sense of the profound moral imperatives of a faithful married life. Some may have only an awkward and mechanical personal prayer life - yet they keep outwardly a regular presence at Mass. For all the power of the Eucharist, being as it is the gift of the whole Christ in His real and substantial presence, still the Eucharist is not magic and its grace requires our right reception. These Catholics, failing to hold to the fullness of dimension of a genuine life in Christ, fail also to bear good witness or to be good example for us.

So also some Catholics can fail a full embrace of the faith by seeking only a rigidly correct moral life, or by seeking only an inner and individualistic relationship with God in prayer. Life in Christ is genuinely life - the Christian life is fully human, enabled by divine grace - we cannot take only part of a life. Life demands its integrity and wholeness. A Catholic beginning his life of discipleship, beginning his celebration of this great and beautiful liturgy of Christ within, must set his heart upon the fullness of the call. Even now, in the beginning of the beginning, let us set our hearts toward greatness in Christ! Let us allow our hearts to hope for true holiness, to yearn for all that He has for us, to desire to offer our all, our very best, to Him and His Gospel.

The call to guard this new life

Thomas Aquinas notes that the intention of a soul in the beginning of the spiritual life, in the stage of the beginner, must be to guard and protect the charity he has now received because of Baptism. How precious is this gift! Christians may not even realize what they have received in Baptism, if their formation and preparation was poor. In Baptism, the new Christian receives grace by infusion into his soul, grace which is a share and participation in the holy life of God! This grace sanctifies the human person, bringing forgiveness of all sin - original sin and all personal sins, taking away all need for any punishment for any sin. What magnificent divine work is Baptism! This grace brings divine adoption into sonship, translating the soul out of the old Adam and into Christ Jesus the Son.

We begin to see, therefore, the significance and meaning of the three petitions of the *Our Father* that mark the three stations of the first movement of the interior liturgy - "deliver us from evil," "lead us not into temptation," and "forgive us our trespasses as we forgive those who trespass against us." These are the prayers of the heart given by Christ to especially help the soul in this first movement of His saving work. These are the petitions given to help the person turn away from the dark evil of his former life, help him through the struggles of temptation that will assault him, and enable him to face the hardness of heart within him - the hardness that will stop the interior liturgy if he does not open his heart to the living mercies of God.

The beginning of the life of prayer

The inner gift of God's grace is the first word of a dialogue meant to last into eternity - the dialogue of prayer with God. He begins this dialogue with the gift of His grace, but then continues it in what usually appears to be a long period of silence! Yet it is a silence in which He shows us, again and again, His great love for us. He may not speak, but He answers our prayer time after time, in surprising ways. He gives us in His own way the assurance of His nearness and His love.

Catholic understanding of prayer includes two major divisions or categories: first there is ascetical prayer, then mystical or contemplative prayer. Mystical prayer is a characteristic of the second movement of the interior liturgy. In the first movement of the interior liturgy our life of prayer begins at the beginning, with ascetical prayer. Prayer that is called ascetical is called this because it is prayer that we can do, in the ordinary grace of our Baptism. It is also the prayer that we must do and persevere in, if we are to remain in the grace we have been given. Ascetical prayer has several traditional levels, or grades, or stages. There is first vocal prayer, which then can develop into meditation or mental prayer, which can then mature to become affective prayer. Affective prayer, if it matures and develops, grows or settles into what may be called the prayer of simplicity.[42] These grades of ascetical prayer then are essentially three: vocal prayer, meditation (affective prayer being a form of meditation) and the prayer of simplicity. This last grade of prayer is also sometimes known as the prayer of recollection, and even acquired contemplation, distinct from infused contemplation.

Prayer in this first movement, the liturgy of the word, begins with vocal prayer - our words, either recited from a formula prayer of the Church, or our own personal thoughts and hopes and desires, called spontaneous prayer. We begin our life of prayer with words, in this work of Christ within us, the interior liturgy of the Word. We pray to God whom we know from His words in sacred revelation, revealing to us The Word, the Son.

A crucially important formula prayer for us, of course, is the *Our Father*. Also the *Hail Mary*, the *Glory Be*, and many others in the tradition of the Church are beautiful, safe and rich formula prayers. Spontaneous vocal prayer may seem at first difficult: we may feel awkward and self-conscious in our attempts to actually speak to God. Spontaneous prayer allows us to express in personally meaningful ways the actual desires of the heart, our personal needs and desires, our fears and our hopes. It is not uncommon for spontaneous prayer, in the beginning, to be concerned with the smaller circle of the needs of the self and one's immediate family. Later in time, and especially in the later movements of the interior liturgy beyond the first, spontaneous prayer can develop to include the needs of the larger realm of the Church, and the world of the lost and the dying.

Vocal prayer, which begins in the first station of the liturgy and continues throughout our life of prayer, is intended to develop and expand to meditation. Meditation, simply, is the engagement of the mind with some revealed truth of God, with the intention to obey in love the truth that we hear. Said another way, meditation is intentional listening to revealed truth, that we might know the truth of God, and knowing, that we might love the truth of God, and loving we might live the truth of God. This is our vocation: God made us to know Him, to love Him, to serve Him in this world and to be happy with Him in the next.

Meditation, prayed well, becomes simplified and warmed into affective prayer, which simplifies still more to the quiet rest of the prayer of simplicity. In essence, this is a simple and quiet resting before God, and it is a waiting for a movement in prayer that only God can do. In the prayer of simplicity, the soul waits on the Lord in prayer for the initiation of mystical prayer, and infused contemplation.

Chapter 5. The First Station: ... but deliver us from evil.

The Station of Deliverance

The first station of the interior liturgy is the station of deliverance. The prayer here is "deliver us from evil." The sacramental grace here prayed for, and given, is the grace of Baptism. This station corresponds to that first mansion within the soul in the *Interior Castle*, seen by St. Teresa of Avila.[43]

In her description of the first mansions of the interior castle, Teresa described a soul quite weak and vulnerable spiritually. She wrote of a soul still engulfed by the pleasures of the passing world, still absorbed by it, even while having begun to seek God and His life. Such a soul, Teresa wrote, desires not to offend God, and rather to do good works, yet with very little strength. Such a soul needs to grow in self-knowledge, and in an understanding of the actual horror and ugliness of sin. Such a soul cries to be freed from the power of evil. Within such a soul, the interior liturgy has begun at its first station. The prayer most urgently called forth is this, "Deliver us from evil."

This station of deliverance is a gift from the Lord to a soul hungry for His healing, and weary from the struggling apart from Him.

"Come to me, all who labor and are heavy laden, and I will give you rest. Take my yoke upon you, and learn from me; for I am gentle and lowly in heart, and you will find rest for your souls. For my yoke is easy, and my burden is light."[44]

What is the good news of the Gospel? How does Jesus offer us rest? To approach these questions as for the first time, we must hear goodness from the context of evil; we must hear rest from the context of the toil and futility of one outside of His life. To pray, "Deliver us from evil," we need to know the context of evil: the evil one, Satan, the devil.

The Power of Evil

There are many evils in our world, evils from which we cry to be free. There are physical evils: hurricanes, earthquakes, and the scorching heat and body-numbing cold that can kill the poor who are abandoned to them. There are physical diseases such as cancers, brain deterioration, bone degeneration, organ failures, viruses and debilitating or even lethal bacteria. There are moral evils: lust, lying, theft, adultery, murder, deceit, coveting, blasphemy, and so on. There is evil outside of us and there is temptation to evil within us. But all of this evil, both physical and moral, can be traced to the original break of human fellowship with God. When the first human couple believed the lies of Satan over God, and made a moral choice against His eternal truth, all creation fell into subjection to decay. All evil can be traced to his work among the people of God. We must know that our enemy is always, ultimately, the devil. "For we are not contending against flesh and blood, but against the principalities, against the powers, against the world rulers of this present darkness, against the spiritual hosts of wickedness in the heavenly places." (Eph 6:12)

It is paradoxical that in the spiritual realm, we who are dead in sin do not know it. We who are in bondage to evil do not realize how enslaved we are! Some of us assert the opposite: we are free and we choose freely. We claim that we drink excessively because we choose to. We think that our carousing and immorality are expressions of our freedom. We think that we could quit gambling, or other sins, any time we wish: we don't want to stop. The truth remains, in spite of our assertions to the contrary, that we are not free. Not merely our actions, but our very desires are in bondage. We cannot want to stop this sin or that.

There may be some of us who are troubled inwardly, but then we seek to justify our acts as normal. Adultery may be wrong in general, but how can it be wrong for me when it seems so good? Everyone lies on their income tax returns. The company expects us to take home office supplies - it's not really stealing. Abortion is legal - how can it be sinful? I work very hard all week - I deserve a little fun in my free time. What does "pornography" mean anyway? We all have these desires naturally. We lie to ourselves that sin is normal, because sin is not and never can be normal, no matter how common it may be.

Finally, there are those of us who are the "good, normal people". We are not adulterers, or thieves; we rarely depart from simple honesty; we have never killed anyone. Are we in bondage to the devil? Are we slaves of Satan? It is most important to understand the reality of this "good, normal" bondage! It is important for all Christians, in all the stations of interior communion with Christ, to realize the need of the "good, normal" people for the saving truth of Jesus Christ!

And behold, one came up to him, saying, "Teacher, what good deed must I do, to have eternal life?"

And he said to him, "Why do you ask me about what is good? One there is who is good. If you would enter life, keep the commandments." He said to him, "Which?"

And Jesus said, "You shall not kill, You shall not commit adultery, You shall not steal, You shall not bear false witness, honor your father and mother, and, You shall love your neighbor as yourself." The young man said to him, "All these I have observed; what do I still lack?"

Jesus said to him, "If you would be perfect, go, sell what you possess and give to the poor, and you will have treasure in heaven; and come, follow me." When the young man heard this he went away sorrowful; for he had great possessions.

And Jesus said to his disciples, "Truly, I say to you, it will be hard for a rich man to enter the kingdom of heaven. Again I tell you, it is easier for a camel to go through the eye of a needle than for a rich man to enter the kingdom of God." [45]

We are rightly disturbed by this passage, as the disciples were, by this encounter with truth of a good, normal and rich young man. He had found in himself no traces of the evil that would keep him from the eternal life he wanted. He had kept to the moral commandments given to his people by God. "All these I have observed; what do I still lack?" The evil that is death for us does not always manifest itself overtly by murders, or thefts, or adulteries as we understand them. There is the evil one, an angelic person – the devil – who has his own spiritual powers as well as his other evil angels to assist him. There is the moral evil that is sin, chosen and enacted by human persons. There is, as well, a personal subjective compromise with evil that keeps a "good" person apart from God and His saving will. This rich young man chose the "good" he thought he had in his worldly possessions, over the good awaiting him in Christ.

Here is an evil that good people can fail to recognize, or fail to fear as they should: the evil of loving lesser goods over the greatest good. This is the subtle evil of the familiar and the customary, the evil of the good hand or eye that offends[46], the evil of the old wineskins.[47] Evil is anything that keeps a human person apart from the life of Christ! We are to be eager to leave anything, any person, any place any time for the overwhelming good awaiting us in Jesus Christ! Peter was able to say, speaking for all the disciples, "we have left everything and followed you."[48]

The young man in the story believes that he had kept all the commandments listed by Jesus – but had he kept the first, from which all the others flow? Jesus was once asked on another occasion, "Which commandment is the first of all?" (Mk 12:28)

> Jesus answered, "The first is, 'Hear, O Israel: The Lord our God, the Lord is one; and you shall love the Lord your God

with all your heart, and with all your soul, and with all your mind, and with all your strength.' The second is this, 'You shall love your neighbor as yourself.' There is no other commandment greater than these."

And the scribe said to him, "You are right, Teacher; you have truly said that he is one, and there is no other but he; and to love him with all the heart, and with all the understanding, and with all the strength, and to love one's neighbor as oneself, is much more than all whole burnt offerings and sacrifices."

And when Jesus saw that he answered wisely, he said to him, "You are not far from the kingdom of God."[49]

We must listen attentively to this word from Jesus, because it contradicts common belief. The crucial commandments are not negatives, they are more fundamental than mere sinful acts to avoid. Sin is the fruit of darkness, it follows from the failure to love. Evil dwells where God is not the wholly beloved Lord in a human heart.

The petition, "Deliver us from evil," is part of the prayer essential to the life of prayer of every human person. Every person is either in immediate personal need of this deliverance - "Father God, deliver me from evil!" - or he is under obligation by love to pray this for the millions of souls, brothers and sisters, who are so enslaved - "Father, deliver us from evil."

We run from the truth. We deny, we claim innocence, we claim freedom, we claim justification - we refuse to see or hear the truth. Why? Perhaps because without real hope, the truth itself is too terrible, too dark, too deadly. If I am dead in sin, then what hope can there be for me? If I do not really have freedom, then I am not even myself. If I am truly in bondage to Satan, heading to an eternity in hell, then the only human response is total and utter despair. To see the horrible truth of our death in sin is too horrible to even consider apart from the hope made possible in the Good News. Without Gospel hope, but with only the knowledge of our bondage to evil, even suicide would not be able to quench the torture of my human existence.

Gospel truth does set us free! The good news of Jesus sets in the human heart a hope, a light that is at the same time beautiful and terrible. It is awesome: it enkindles an awe and a fear in the soul that is at once clear, beautiful, and true. To begin to appreciate the goodness of the good news, we need to consider more deeply the tragedy of the alternative. The power of the evil one, from whom we find deliverance in Jesus Christ, is founded upon the lies of "the father of lies," this one "who was a murderer from the beginning." (Jn 8:44) His power over us ultimately is founded upon our fear of death.

> Since therefore the children share in flesh and blood, he himself likewise partook of the same nature, that through death he might destroy him who has the power of death, that is, the devil, and deliver all those who through fear of death were subject to lifelong bondage.[50]

The importance and the implications of this verse are difficult to overstate. What has subjected us to lifelong bondage? It is our fear, and specifically our fear of death. What frees us from this bondage to the devil? When we are no longer fearful of death, the devil no longer has any power over us. It is "through fear of death" that we "were subject to lifelong bondage."

Gospel power

When we are free of fear, we are free of bondage. This is the overwhelming power of the resurrection of Jesus Christ, which fills us with hope for our own resurrection on the last day. Because of the resurrection, death is not the last word! Because of the resurrection, death is not the end: we can live and we can die in hope.

This simple truth of the power of the fear of death over us

is itself significant and helpful. Because we fear death so, we grasp blindly in the darkness of a limited existence, a mere candle in the night. We clutch at pleasures and consolations all destined to be taken away, we grasp for the brief good available for us, always in the dark belief that it is all to be lost – it is all like sand running between our fingers. So eat, drink and be merry, for tomorrow we die. So we grab what we can, knowing that all is futile and only the infinite blackness of extinction awaits us. In this way, we give our souls to self-indulgence, to despair, to the evil father of lies.

The truth of Christ contradicts all these lies! Jesus loved, and shared, and gave, and was good and righteous and holy! He did not turn into Himself: He lived in truth before His Father God. He did not avoid or escape the judgment of God upon mankind for its sin, even in His sinless purity. He offered Himself up to death, even death on a cross, and He proved the love of God for us all even in our very real sins. In the truth of His resurrection, He made void the claim of Satan upon mankind. Death is not the end. Love and life are our destiny.

Will we believe the Good News? Will we see, in the light of Christ, the empty claim of Satan and his impotence now over us? Will we receive the deliverance from evil for which we pray in this petition? Deliverance is given! We are free! Jesus has overcome the devil, and the power of death! Therefore repent, and believe the Good News!

Evil subtle and civilized

There are evils that have become so integrated into our culture in the West, that a Christian might become blind to them. Here in the first station of the interior liturgy, the Christian must truly see these evils, and he must turn from them. This turning from evil, with the prayer "deliver us from evil," must be strong and definitive – even though, in this first of seven stations, the deliverance will not yet be complete. Here the liturgy begins: here Christ begins in us, to shepherd us out of a land of darkness and into His marvelous light.

His grace awakens us to the reality and the danger of the evils that this culture hardly considers evil anymore, because these desires and actions have become so common. We know that murder is evil! Yet abortion is legal, and sadly common, and this mindset is now branching or has now branched to include the elimination of another "undesirable" group, the elderly and the sick, through euthanasia. We know that adultery is evil! Or is it, in our society today? Sexual immorality has become so commonplace, so widespread throughout the culture, that it does not surprise anyone anymore. But it should trouble us deeply! Sexual immorality is most serious, and is lethal to the soul of a disciple.

Although it has become so commonplace, the Christian must flee all sexual immorality. In this culture we have separated sexuality from covenant love, and so it has degenerated to mere individual pleasure. Robbed of its true dignity and sacred character, improper sexuality saturates our culture like pollution in the air: it is everywhere, permeating the society and distorting our senses of what is appropriate and wholesome and worthy of human persons. With each new generation, it seems, sexual awareness dips to a younger and younger group, as do sexual activity, promiscuity and the resultant sexual diseases. Our children are losing their childhood. Our culture is losing a sense of the real meaning and importance of human sexuality, and indeed a sense of humanity itself – what it means to be a human person. The beginner in the spiritual life must hold fast to holiness, to sexual purity, to a chaste life as a married or as a single person.

Sexual morality is intimately linked to the Gospel of Life. Life becomes cheaper and cheaper, as love becomes more distant, and the human heart becomes colder and harder. Unwanted and "inconvenient" children are killed, legally and illegally. Some would want to allow abortion even as the child is being born! And such unnatural and criminal "laws" have actually been supported and endorsed by Catholic legislators! Children are abandoned to day care and television; teens are raised and guided by strangers or by one another; families are dissolved and scattered under the pressures of a society that produces in order to consume, and consumes in a futile search for happiness. We have fallen so far into darkness that many of the weak and uninformed cannot see those lights that still endure. The beginner in the spiritual life must hold fast to the gospel of life, seeing in all life the precious gift in the image of God.

In a culture more and more dehumanized, we have turned to material idols to substitute for our needed communion in the living God. What we have begun to call "life" becomes more and more expensive. Many people are deeply in debt, drunk with gadgets and things and toys and fashions, instantly available, with easy credit and "no money down." Unable to find the real treasures of human life, we have abandoned ourselves to the cheap trinkets of the consumer society. And they have enslaved us. The beginner in the spiritual life must hold fast to financial responsibility, springing as it does from the kingship we are given in Christ, as stewards of this garden.

Financial bondage, through excessive and overwhelming debt, is not the only form of bondage that is common in our society. Human persons, blindly seeking life, liberty and happiness in the wrong places, have fallen into the abuse of alcohol, of drugs, of foods, of gambling, of sexuality, of things - and of other persons as though they also were "things." Our true happiness is found only in God - and if not found there, we will never be happy. The beginner, in this first station of the interior liturgy, needs to turn away from all sins, and turn to God.

Poverty, Chastity and Obedience

The evangelical virtues of poverty, chastity and obedience are embraced with vows among consecrated religious. They can help us all, however, to see more clearly into the life to which we all are called. Not necessarily poverty, but responsible use of material goods; not necessarily celibacy, but chastity and sexual holiness whether married or single; and not necessarily obedience as to a religious superior, but faithful obedience to Christ and to His Church in His name – these virtues can enlighten life for us all. Especially to us in the first station of the interior liturgy, these three virtues can help us to see a path of sanity through the chaos of this culture.

We must, in the first station, begin to say "no" to sin and "yes" to God and to His way in our lives. Material over-consumption is all around us; we need to learn balance and reasonableness in the use of material goods. We need the guiding light of a sense of true Gospel "poverty", that we may begin to grow rich in the things of God. Sexual abuse and self-indulgence deeply permeate and saturate the secular culture; we need to learn the meaning of chastity and the true meaning of sexual intimacy. Disobedience, irreverence and an independent spirit are exalted to almost mythic status in our society; we need to learn the place and value of submission to the truth.

The subtle and civilized evils so common in our culture branch from a core denial of love – or, to look at it another way, from a self-centered and self-indulgent attitude that blinds us to our true dignity and vocation. This attitude that exalts the individual self, at almost any cost, has resulted in a society that is desperately poor in love, love that is most important to life. Love calls us to self-surrender, self-offering, self-gift. Love is the

opposite of self-indulgence, and self-gratification, and self-centeredness. In a culture that exalts individualism and self-fulfill-
ment, it is not surprising that we have trouble with loving.

Poverty, chastity and obedience can become lights for us, as
we seek to turn away from the subtle and ever-present temptations around us: temptations to self-indulgence and self-glorifi-
cation, temptations away from the work, the risk and the
investment of love.

Baptism - the Sacrament of the First Station

The sacrament that specifically illuminates this station,
revealing its meaning, is the sacrament of Baptism. The interior
liturgy begins in darkness: while we were yet in sin, He loved
us. We were dead to Him, yet He lives and His life is pure and
eternal love. He reached into our darkness with loving grace,
hidden and unrecognized grace, unreturned love. God calls us
in a language we did not expect, through signs we did not
understand. The interior liturgy begins with His call to us yet
in bondage to sin, and step by step He leads us to a home we
never knew we had, into a communion of love we did not
know that we longed for.

He called us. We understood very little, yet we followed
Him. We received Baptism, the sacrament of faith, and with
this grace - a participation in the very life of God! - we are
born anew and we begin a wholly new life and journey on this
earth, a journey toward blessed communion in the Holy
Trinity, in the beatitude we call the beatific vision.

Thus begins the interior liturgy: our inner participation in
the saving work of Christ - a participation, although interior,
that has by necessity its exterior, human expressions and man-
ifestations. Our first "yes" to God is expressed in Baptism, and
in the dynamic of baptismal grace we are in fact delivered from

the bondage of evil. In the grace of Baptism we are forgiven all sin, original and personal, and infused with sanctifying grace that makes us children of God and heirs with Christ in the kingdom. We are given the virtues - even though initially in potential and seed form - of faith and hope and charity. We are given life - a life intended to grow in holiness and charity, leading in fellowship with the saints to the divine communion of heaven. Baptism is the sacrament of faith - the sacrament of repentance and rejection of the ways of evil, to and into the life in Christ with His saints in the Church.

Baptism is the sacrament of entry into the Christian life, as this first station is the beginning of the interior liturgy of the work of Christ in the soul. Baptism begins to answer the great, profound questions of human life and vocation: "Who am I?" "Who am I called to be?" Baptism is the sacrament of cleansing freedom from sin, the grace from God that answers the plea, "deliver us from evil!" Baptism is "the door which gives access to the other sacraments,"[51] as this first station is the entry into the whole of the interior liturgy, the beginning of the pilgrimage of the Christian life.

Baptism begins our consecration to the Christian life in the world. We may not fully realize, or appreciate, this consecration at this point. In the second movement of the interior liturgy, called the liturgy of consecration, this self-offering becomes experiential: yet it begins here with Baptism. Our concern must be faithfulness to this new life! Evil is still very near; the old ways are close at hand. Fortitude is needed. The grace - God's present help - is available for us, in the grace of the sacrament of Baptism; we must stay close to Him and His grace! In practical terms, this means we must say "no" to the old ways, and "yes" to the new, every day and many times in the day. This is no theoretical challenge before us: we face a struggle against principalities and powers far beyond our own mere strength.

Success in this first station of the interior liturgy is not guaranteed. Failure is a real human possibility. A human person, called out from the darkness of evil, of sin and of death, can fall back again. We must pray with all the resolve, the courage, the faith and the sincerity that we can muster! We pray, "deliver us from evil!" In the first two of the stations of the interior liturgy, we often mean only "deliver me from evil!" This is sufficient to call out the abundant grace and mercy of God, who wills our salvation a million times more than we do. We pray "deliver us," yet we can scarcely see beyond our own personal need. God does not condemn us for this, but rather He loves and nurtures us, building us toward His holy and perfect intention.

The grace of Baptism, then, crucially important to every Christian, is particularly significant to the Christian in the first station of the interior liturgy. For the Christian just beginning a life of discipleship, of following Christ, the first graces of Baptism are acutely and urgently needed. It is important to the Christian at this stage of his life in Christ to keep close to his baptismal graces: to guard them and treasure them. How do we do this? Listening carefully to the *Catechism* presentation on this sacrament, growing in understanding of all that it means for us, we can begin to treasure this great gift as we ought, as Baptism itself deserves.

Grace given in Baptism cleanses us of all sin, and translates us into saving life in Christ. Sin, however, attacks this grace and this life - and sin can destroy it. Even venial sins weaken our life in Christ, and leave us more vulnerable to deadly mortal sin. A single mortal sin brings death to the human soul![52] Sin can be forgiven, through repentance and in the sacrament of Confession, yet we must never become casual in our attitude toward sin. We must decisively turn from sin and evil! We must turn to Christ, and to all that is in Him! Baptism is the grace called forth, in the petition, "Deliver us from evil." In this grace we need to remain.

Our prayer must be persistent; our presence at Mass and any other sacraments must be as frequent as we can arrange. We must be courageous in the face of invitations to sin, steadfastly enduring in the moral life of a Christian as faithfully as we can. We must strive to listen and learn, growing in our understanding of this great faith passed down to us from the apostles. In other words, in the four pillars of the faith - the creed, the sacraments, the moral life, and prayer - we must be faithful and we must grow. "Like newborn babes, long for the pure spiritual milk, that by it you may grow up to salvation; for you have tasted the kindness of the Lord." (1 Pet 2:2-3)

Prayer in the First Station

Prayer in the first station of the interior liturgy is usually vocal prayer, and that, only the beginning first stages of the depths possible in vocal prayer. Vocal prayer is prayer spoken, "vocal", although often we include also prayer thought, or spoken in the heart. Vocal prayers, especially the great formula prayers of the Church - the *Our Father*, the *Hail Mary*, the *Glory Be*, and so on - are easily abused! We can so easily recite them automatically, mindlessly, impersonally. The challenge for us in the beginning first station of the interior liturgy is to pray our vocal prayers authentically, personally.

The formula prayers of the Church offer us a great treasure. Perhaps especially the *Our Father* invites us, in its infinite richness and depth, to be present as we pray: to listen, and intend, and be attentive to what is in truth a dialogue with God. This attentiveness, and the reverent devotion that grows in such attentiveness, will lead us in our prayer to the next level of ascetical prayer: meditation. Meditation is particularly appropriate to the second station of the interior liturgy, and will be considered there.

Prayer, including vocal prayer, is discussed in many other books[53], but some discussion of it here is essential also. It is necessary to stress the personal nature of authentic prayer. It must be I myself, you yourself, pronouncing and intending and meaning the words spoken to God. He created us, He saved us in love, He calls us! God is Personal - the Father, the Son and the Holy Spirit are Persons. Prayer with God demands that we approach Him as persons. If we are to be present to the Lord in our prayer, and not merely mindlessly reciting religious words, we must be present fully as human persons. We must be present in ourselves as we are, before Him who is eternally present, our God. Prayer deserves to be a personal encounter, person to Person. Prayer is indeed communication. All persons deserve our real presence, when we enter conversation with them. If human persons are worthy of our undistracted presence, when we talk with them, then surely God deserves our authentic presence in prayer.

How are we to pray? It may seem that prayer is very simple. Prayer is very simple - prayer is more simple than we are. Because of our complications, our prayer is often a struggle against distractions and preoccupations, a struggle with honesty, a struggle with fears and guilt, and so on. There is a brokenness and a confusion within us. God is calling us out of this darkness and into His simplicity, and He gives us the power, by His grace, to follow Him. Even with grace it is not easy, but He is with us and He will not abandon us even in the darkness He sometimes must permit in the journey.

The requirements of vocal prayer are commonly said to be attention and devotion. These bring to bear the engagement of the mind in attention, and the heart in devotion. The mind and the heart engaged in prayer together suggest the fullness of our presence as persons. We can easily imagine the ways to fall short of this full presence! We are tempted to distraction especially in the well-known formula prayers of the Church such as the *Our Father*. The prayer is so well established in memory that we can recite it without thinking, automatically, while at the same time planning something we need to do after prayer, or making a mental list of items we need at the store, and so on. This is certainly not prayer, lacking both attention and devotion.

Attention, in vocal prayer, requires that I am aware, first, of who is praying - that I have some measure of honest self-knowledge of who I am before God. Second, it requires awareness of the One to whom I am praying: I pray before God Almighty. Third, it requires my awareness of what I am saying, in my prayer: the meaning of the words and what they convey.

Devotion has its component of the mind, of course. Devotion is not merely feelings, but it should include the human feelings appropriate to communion with God who is love. Devotion includes also reverence, springing from a humble heart. Devotion also includes that resolution and intention of the will to do the truth: we have devotion, grounded in the communion of love with eternal God; we exercise devotion in acts appropriate to this communion of love.

Vocal prayer needs attention and devotion, to bring forth the communion in prayer that we seek, and vocal prayer brings forth as a kind of fruit, increased attention and devotion! This is because the beauty and truth we find in authentic prayer, stirs us to hunger even more for more beauty and more truth. The splendor of the truth we find urges us to greater attentiveness that we might find more truth. The joy in devotion that we experience impels us to even greater devotion.

The Our Father in the first station

The *Our Father* is perhaps the first prayer we should begin with, to simply slow down and listen as we pray. We need to become intentional in prayer: to grow in recollection and in presence before God. Praying the *Our Father*, we can begin with slowing down, praying audibly, and listening. What are we saying? What do the words express? What do these words require of me, as I pray them: to what am I committing or obliging myself?

As I begin to really listen to this prayer as I pray it, I discover that the prayer has a potency of its own. Praying "our" Father, pondering "our" and not "my" Father, the whole mystery of God's will for our relationship among men begins to work within me. God wants us to care for one another! God wants us to be brothers and sisters, to live as if we were really brothers and sisters, because we really are! God wants us to pray to "our" Father, realizing that this common bond, this solidarity among all men and women, is the truth of our humanity. It is not only His will that we should obey – it is the truth that life requires.

Phrase by phrase, petition by petition, the prayer unfolds and opens to us, as we slow down and listen. These words are of God, and have power. We speak beyond our lives, beyond our experience – yet grounded in them – we pray beyond ourselves to God, using His own words given to us for us. We pray to our "Father, who art in heaven." We do not understand "heaven", yet the word stirs a hope in us. This world has pleasure, yet also much suffering; every joy and happiness that we find here has a limit and a boundary. We look to a "heaven" that we do not understand, yet hunger for.

The prayer works and forms us, and awakens us to a higher call as we listen and pray. Through the whole prayer, and to the last petition, the prayer re-orders us from within. In the last petition, especially significant in this first station of the interior liturgy, we are awakened to the mortal danger of a way of life we are now called out of forever. There is evil in this world, an evil more powerful than we are apart from Christ, and we need His deliverance. This petition, 'deliver us from evil," has a potency in the soul because of His divine grace; this petition can help bring us to that saving fear that is the beginning of wisdom.

> My son, if you receive my words
>
> and treasure up my commandments with you,
>
> making your ear attentive to wisdom
>
> and inclining your heart to understanding;
>
> yes, if you cry out for insight
>
> and raise your voice for understanding,
>
> if you seek it like silver
>
> and search for it as for hidden treasures;
>
> then you will understand the fear of the LORD
>
> and find the knowledge of God.[54]

Can it be that the "fear of the Lord" is precisely the antidote for us who "through fear of death were subject to lifelong bondage" (Heb 2:15) to the devil? Can it be that one fear is unto bondage and sorrow, while the other fear is unto freedom and peace? These fears are radically different. The fear of the Lord is a holy fear that is due to God the Almighty - a fear that develops from a servile fear of the beginning of faith, into a filial fear with reverence, awe and humility before God our Father. The fear of the Lord is the beginning of our freedom from the power of evil, the beginning of the freedom to be a human person created in the image of God, made for communion and happiness and peace.

Examination of conscience in the first station

I pray for deliverance from evil: do I truly want it? I read in the Bible and in the *Catechism* about sins that are so wrong that they can bring condemnation to hell. Do I really believe this?

Following is an examination of conscience, to reflect upon before the sacrament of Reconciliation, or at other times in prayer. The Ten Commandments (traditional Catholic formulation):

1. <u>I am the LORD your God: you shall not have strange Gods before me.</u>

I pray to "our Father who art in heaven," but are there other gods in my life? Do I chase after pleasure as a god? Do I value my own reputation among men above God's law? Do I honor God among all my friends, and when I am alone?

2. <u>You shall not take the name of the LORD your God in vain.</u>

I pray, "Hallowed be thy name," but do I use God's name wrongly - cursing in anger, swearing on His name about trivial matters, or in jokes and casual conversation?

3. <u>Remember to keep holy the LORD'S Day.</u>

I pray, "Thy kingdom come," but do I follow the laws of His kingdom? Do I attend Mass when I should? Do I try to be attentive and devout at Mass? Do I refrain from unnecessary servile work on Sundays? Do I try to use Sundays for wholesome and worthy activities? Do I try especially to honor God on Sundays?

4. <u>Honor your father and your mother.</u>

I pray, "Thy will be done," but do I live according to the

will of God as I know it? Do I honor my parents? Do I teach my children to honor their parents? Do I honor all legitimate authority?

5. You shall not kill.

God's will is for life; Jesus came to give life, and life abundantly. Am I truly pro-life? I pray that His will "be done on earth": do I live the gospel of life privately and publicly? Do I consistently support respect for life, and an end to abortion and euthanasia and contraception?

6. You shall not commit adultery.

I pray that His will "be done on earth as it is in heaven." Do I seek the holiness and purity of heart that does live His life? Do I violate the marriage covenant in any way? Do I sin sexually by adultery, or fornication, or masturbation, or through any inappropriate genital acts?

7. You shall not steal.

I pray to "our" Father, but do I violate my brotherhood in God's people by stealing from my own family? I pray "Deliver us from evil," but do I inflict evil upon others by stealing from them? Do I steal from my place of work and then seek to justify it to myself falsely? Do I steal from my employer, by wasting time he has paid me to work?

8. You shall not bear false witness against your neighbor.

I pray "Deliver us from evil," but do I inflict evil upon others by lying about them? Do I steal from their reputation with gossip or slander or subtle insinuation?

9. You shall not covet your neighbor's wife.

I pray, "Lead us not into temptation," but do I feed into temptation by clinging to improper thoughts and desires for another man's wife, or another woman's husband? Do I watch fantasies in movies or television, or in books or magazines, that lead me to improper sexual desires?

10. You shall not covet your neighbor's goods.

I pray, "Lead us not into temptation," but do I open my heart and mind to covetous desire for things through the advertising of the mass media? Do I invite into my heart the false promises that the advertisers use, to make me think that if I could only own this or that, I would be happy? Do I fail to believe and live God's promise for the "daily bread" that we need, to discover our true vocation?

Prayer:
Most Holy God, our Father,

You gave us your law through your servant Moses; you gave us grace and life through your Son, Jesus Christ. Open our ears, to hear your law. Open our hearts to the grace of obedience, in Christ Jesus. Deliver us all, we pray, from the lies of the evil one.

St. Michael the Archangel, defend us in battle. Be our protection against the wickedness and snares of the devil. May God rebuke him, we humbly pray, and do thou, O Prince of the Heavenly Host, cast into hell Satan and all the evil spirits who wander throughout this world seeking the ruin of souls.

Amen.

Chapter 6. The Second Station: Lead us not into temptation....

The Station of Trial

The second station of the interior liturgy is the station of trial and temptations. The prayer here is, "Lead us not into temptation." The sacramental grace here prayed for, and given, is the grace of Confirmation. This station corresponds to that second mansion within the soul in the *Interior Castle*, seen by St. Teresa of Avila.[55]

In her writing of the second mansions of the interior castle, Teresa described a soul who desires to advance in the inner life, and in fidelity to Christ, yet still having vulnerabilities to sin. The particular weakness and susceptibility here, is that the soul is only beginning to realize the dangers of near occasions of sin. Perseverance is most urgently needed, when the evil one fills the mind with temptations and enticements to return to the ways of sin. Persons here understand the need to grow, and to move further in faith, yet they are only beginning to be aware of the real threat of temptation. Within such a soul, the interior liturgy has moved into its second station. The prayer most urgently called forth, therefore, is this petition, "Lead us not into temptation."

In this station of the liturgy, the soul learns something of himself, and his inner weaknesses.

And he said, "What comes out of a man is what defiles a man. For from within, out of the heart of man, come evil thoughts, fornication, theft, murder, adultery, coveting, wickedness, deceit, licentiousness, envy, slander, pride, foolishness. All these evil things come from within, and they defile a man."[56]

This, the second station, marks progress in the interior liturgy toward a more interior and more personal confronta-

tion with evil. Here there is a more interior engagement of the
self in this struggle against evil, than in the first and previous
station. In the first station, the soul prayed for deliverance from
evil, and specifically from the evil one. Here, the battle moves
inward to a trial within the heart: the battle of temptation.

The person who enters this second station has made
progress in the interior liturgy. Some victory over the power of
evil has been achieved, and therefore a certain confidence and
assurance is warranted. Great danger remains, however,
because in spite of the knowledge that in Christ there is victory
over the evil one, still there is the possibility of choosing to
leave our safe harbor in Christ. Now, we realize the strength
we are given in faith, yet we begin to learn of our freedom nevertheless to choose to turn away from saving faith. We begin
to realize that temptation to sin is a continuing and personal
struggle. Christ has won the battle! Yet I can choose to remain
in Him, or I can prefer the lures and enticements of sin.

The sacrament of the first station of the liturgy is Baptism,
which is a complete cleansing from all sin:

> By Baptism all sins are forgiven, original sin and all personal
> sins, as well as all punishment for sin. In those who have been
> reborn nothing remains that would impede their entry into
> the Kingdom of God, neither Adam's sin, nor personal sin,
> nor the consequences of sin, the gravest of which is separation
> from God.[57]

After Baptism there remains, however, in the Christian a
certain "inclination to sin", called concupiscence.
Concupiscence is not itself sin, but it is a certain weakness and
vulnerability, and an attraction to sin which allows us to be
tempted. Concupiscence "is left for us to wrestle with", "it cannot harm those who do not consent but manfully resist it by
the grace of Jesus Christ."[58]

In this second station of the interior liturgy the Christian is called to confront this attraction to sin, this vulnerability to the evil one. We pray, "Lead us not into temptation." The *Catechism* makes clear a possible confusion in this petition: God is not the source of temptation! God will not lead us into temptation – but He will allow us to consent to it, if we choose. The *Catechism* explains the Greek that we translate into English as "lead us":

> It is difficult to translate the Greek verb used by a single English word: the Greek means both "do not allow us to enter into temptation" and "do not let us yield to temptation." (Cf. Mt 26 41) "God cannot be tempted by evil and he himself tempts no one"(James 1:13); on the contrary, he wants to set us free from evil. We ask him not to allow us to take the way that leads to sin.[59]

This petition of the *Our Father* is crucially important to the Christian, so recently freed from the dominion of evil. Evil must be refused interiorly! We must, in sober self-awareness of our own attraction to sin, resist. This is the concern of the Christian in the second station of the interior liturgy: to engage the enemy within, to confront our own sinful desires lurking inside of us. Here also we discover the gift of this engagement! It is for our good that God allows our faith to be tested.

> Count it all joy, my brethren, when you meet various trials, for you know that the testing of your faith produces steadfastness. And let steadfastness have its full effect, that you may be perfect and complete, lacking in nothing.
>
> If any of you lacks wisdom, let him ask God, who gives to all men generously and without reproaching, and it will be given him. But let him ask in faith, with no doubting, for he who doubts is like a wave of the sea that is driven and tossed by the wind. For that person must not suppose that a double-minded man, unstable in all his ways, will receive anything from the Lord.[60]

If these temptations did not assail us, how would we ever discover the possibility of double-mindedness within us? Without the grace of God in the midst of trial, how would we ever uncover the common human desire to compromise with evil? There is a common weakness in us, seeking to love God and at the same time love the world that contradicts God. We want to have it both ways! The man wants to have his wife and family, and at the same time his adulterous affair. We cherish the law of God, except when we want to do otherwise. We love our Catholic faith - except when it is inconvenient. We want to follow Christ - but not always, not to the cross. We need trials, to test us and to reveal us to ourselves.

> Blessed is the man who endures trial, for when he has stood the test he will receive the crown of life which God has promised to those who love him. Let no one say when he is tempted, "I am tempted by God"; for God cannot be tempted with evil and he himself tempts no one; but each person is tempted when he is lured and enticed by his own desire. Then desire when it has conceived gives birth to sin; and sin when it is full-grown brings forth death.[61]

The *Catechism* helps us to see the "decision of the heart"[62] enabled by temptation. A trial gives us the experience of temptation - trials provide the situation for wrongful desires of the heart to come forward and tempt us. Then, in the light of grace, we can see into our own darkness - and, perhaps weeping and shameful, our love for God can grow. Evil desire is not for our good! And neither can we serve two masters, or continue in double-mindedness. God deserves a whole heart, a single mind, a soul resting in integrity, a human person committed with all his strength to the ways of God that are true.

Insight into our own hearts and desires is necessary. Self-knowledge is necessary, for a person growing in the spiritual life. God gives us the opportunity to grow in this self-knowledge, and to grow also in fortitude and perseverance, through the experience of temptation. In this way, God works it to our good. God is Himself not the source of temptation within us - we are tempted by our own wrongful desires - yet God works even these to our good.

Confirmation - the Sacrament of the Second Station

The sacrament appropriate to this second station of the interior liturgy is the sacrament of Confirmation, the sacrament that enriches the baptized Christian "with a special strength of the Holy Spirit."[63] The *Catechism* lists several ways in which Confirmation strengthens the Christian:

> From this fact, Confirmation brings an increase and deepening of baptismal grace: - it roots us more deeply in the divine filiation which makes us cry, "Abba! Father!";
>
> - It unites us more firmly to Christ;
>
> - it increases the gifts of the Holy Spirit in us;
>
> - it renders our bond with the Church more perfect;
>
> - it gives us a special strength of the Holy Spirit to spread and defend the faith by word and action as true witnesses of Christ, to confess the name of Christ boldly, and never to be ashamed of the Cross....[64]

Confirmation is associated primarily with the exterior expression of our faith - the strength to be His witnesses. Yet this outward expression requires first an inner strength against the temptations to run from His cross. Decision of the heart is necessary for a witness of the faith: "Who, finally, am I to be in my life?" Faithful endurance outwardly in the Christian life demands the interior fidelity to Him proven through the many temptations that will assault the believer. Our prayer, in the second station of this liturgy, is for strength in the trial: "Lead us not into temptation." Temptations call for the graces particularly of the sacrament of Confirmation.

The graces and strength of both Baptism and Confirmation must be guarded, valued and personally engaged in the trials of this second station of the interior liturgy. We must remember the treasure we were given! We must remem-

ber who we are, and who we are called to be! When we are
tempted to succumb to the way that seems easier - although
in truth it is not - we can call upon the strength and power available to us in the grace of our Confirmation. That power of
Confirmation is still there for us, unless we have so sinned
against it that we have lost the graces it gave - and even then
the power can be restored through Confession. We must not
neglect the grace for us in the sacrament, because it is needed in
this time of temptation.

Prayer in the Second Station

Because of this encounter of the heart with temptation,
forcing decision and requiring discernment, the second station
of the interior liturgy can be thought of as the beginning of
the interior life. The interior life will deepen further, and con-
siderably, in the third station, with true self-judgment of the
heart. Yet here in the second station the interior dialogue
begins, in a sense - a dialogue with oneself, with one's desires
and choices. In the context of this new self-awareness,
enabled by grace in the midst of temptation, decisions of the
heart that begin to define oneself begin in earnest.

In this beginning of the interior life, growth in prayer is
appropriate and necessary. In the first station of the interior
liturgy, vocal prayer is usually enough to satisfy the felt needs
of the heart - the needs to keep far from sin, and to remain
close to Christ and His Church. The second station of the
interior liturgy, however, introduces the person through the
interior dialogue of heart-decision, to deeper questions about
oneself, and about this Person Jesus Christ whom I follow.
The more demanding prayer of Christian meditation may
seem to be too much to the beginner in the first station, but
to the disciple proceeding to the second station, meditation is
exactly appropriate.

Meditation seeks a greater understanding of self, of truth, of Church and of Christ. Christian meditation does not end with understanding only - to be authentically Christian meditation, it leads through understanding to faithful obedience to the truth. The "decision of the heart" enabled by the second station, by temptation, stirs the heart to understand the truths now called into question by these temptations. Meditation, in other words, is particularly significant and appropriate to the second station.

Meditation is the intentional engagement of the mind with some truth of God, for the purpose of knowing God more truly, in order to love God more wholeheartedly, in order to serve Him more faithfully in this world and to be happy with Him forever in the next. Meditation is distinctively Christian when it is ordered in this way to the obedience of faith. It is certainly not the emptying of the mind, following some Eastern religion or practice. Also clearly it is not a merely intellectual exercise - meditation is directed always to the obedience of faith, or at least to the sincere resolution to be obedient in all that the soul receives in the light of the prayer. Although there are several schools or methodologies of Christian meditation, all contain the essential elements: 1) the engagement of the mind with divine truth, 2) an examination of one's life in the light of that truth, and 3) the resolution to act according to that truth.[65]

The fruit of meditation is needed by the soul undergoing the trials of temptations. The decisions of the heart need the light of truth, in order to discern rightly. The heart was made to love truth, and to resolve to live truth, once it recognizes the truth through the discernment of the mind and conscience. The decision of the heart, moreover, intending to live the faith in personal and human ways, needs the fortitude of grace - in particular the grace of Confirmation - to live that truth in the world. These all need to come together in this station: grace, meditation, resolution, obedience.

The Christian who would continue with the Lord in this great interior work, and who would not fall back to linger or even to stagnate in the first station of the liturgy, needs to grow in his prayer to include meditation. We never outgrow vocal prayer, but to continue in the interior liturgy we need to expand the meaning of our prayer to also include this development. Meditation is a normal development of vocal prayer, a growth toward a deeper and more personal communion with God than has been experienced so far in vocal prayer only. When the prayer life of a Christian expands so as to include meditation, the Christian will in his times of vocal prayer as well as in his time of meditation experience a more authentic sense of communication with the Lord. Meditation brings light to vocal prayer also! Meditation brings also the warmth of genuine affection to all of the interior life of prayer, especially when it grows further to the stage of meditation called affective prayer.[66]

Sources for meditation should be chosen carefully. The two substantial and trustworthy sources that are best are also easy to find: Scripture and the *Catechism*. Both of these sources are rich in the revelations God has passed on to us; both contain substantial spiritual food. Secondary sources, which are helpful or even needed to help us understand the truth revealed to the Church, call for a careful discernment. Some Scripture commentaries are helpful and beautiful, while others might be dangerous or misleading. Some opinions that we might read on Church doctrine are helpful and useful, while others might be confusing or wrong.

Meditation is concerned with truth, so we must be careful whenever mere human opinions come alongside the revealed truth of God. Here, we as Catholics can be especially grateful for the magisterium of the Church: the trustworthy teaching authority in the Church is given to us precisely to protect us from the confusion we would otherwise have. Encyclicals and other documents of the popes, approved statements of the Vatican officials, writings of our bishops in union with the pope, and the vast treasure of the fathers and doctors and saints of the Church give us an abundant reserve of material for meditation on divine truth.

The Our Father in the second station

The rich meaning in the *Our Father* is more accessible now in this second station, because of the added prayer dimensions of meditation. We can meditate upon this prayer as a whole, or upon any particular petition of the prayer, for years unlimited. We would never reach the end of the mystery, and beauty, and truth of this prayer if we were to prayerfully ponder it for the rest of our lives. Whatever periods of prayerful meditation we can entrust to this prayer and its truth, there will be brought forth much fruit for us. We cannot deplete the prayer given to us by the Lord Himself, nor can we exhaust its meaning - we can only be enriched by it.

The *Catechism* gives us several paragraphs of substantial and trustworthy commentary on each part of this prayer. The *Catechism* includes a background of references in its commentary, to Scripture as well as to other writings from the Church. Each section in the *Catechism*, presenting on the particular parts of the prayer, holds for us therefore much content for our meditation as we probe into the beautiful mystery of this prayer. Phrase by phrase, petition by petition, we can ponder and seek to penetrate into the fullness that He has given us in the *Our Father*. Meditation upon this prayer will help to illuminate the times we will simply pray the prayer, whether in Church liturgies or in solitude.

Mary in the second station

Another meditation that can be helpful and even important to the second station is the rosary. This ancient and traditional prayer brings together both vocal prayer and scriptural
meditation upon the holy mysteries of the great liturgy of salvation. For the beginner not familiar with the Bible, or with
the scriptural foundations of the mysteries of the rosary, this
is the introduction to a wonderful devotion: to the Holy Word
of God in the Bible. The rosary does not include the whole of
Scripture, but in the sacred mysteries that it does celebrate, it
allows the power of the Word of God to form us in a unique
and powerful way.

Scripture is crucial to the spiritual life: we need the Word
of God, we need to grow to love the Word of God. Scripture
testifies, "faith comes from what is heard, and what is heard
comes through the word of Christ." (Rom 10:17, NAB) The
Apostle John explains his Gospel with what might be considered the foundational reason for every work of Scripture:
"...these are written that you may believe that Jesus is the
Christ, the Son of God, and that believing you may have life
in his name." (Jn 20:31)

The rosary is a unique meditation, bringing together so to
speak two dimensions in prayer: the repetitive sequence of the
Our Father, the *Hail Mary* prayers and so on, together with
reflection upon the mysteries of salvation: the annunciation,
the visitation, the birth, and so on. The combined effect of this
prayer-meditation is somewhat similar to the effect of a song,
bringing together the two "dimensions" of both music and
lyrics.

It is possible for a casual listener of a song being sung,
for example, to be aware of only the music - perhaps he likes
the music and begins to hum or whistle along with the melody

of the song, and is unaware of and uninterested in the words or the meanings of the words that comprise the song. Someone else, perhaps, hears the music and appreciates it but appreciates it more because of the words. The music modifies and colors the words with the emotional tones that the music can communicate, while the words add depth, intelligibility and meaning to the effect of the music. The music adds to the words, and the words add to the music in such a way that the combined effect is mysteriously greater, somehow, than the mere sum of its parts.

The rosary, similarly, adds a dimension to the formula vocal prayers and to the meditation upon the mysteries that magnifies both. It is possible for a beginner with the rosary to listen mainly to the formula prayers: the *Our Father*, the ten *Hail Marys*, the *Glory Be*, and so on, much as someone might listen only to the music of a song and not attend at all to the lyrics. So also this person might think only very briefly of the particular mystery of the decade if at all, perhaps at the beginning of the decade, but then forget it entirely and be conscious for the rest of the decade of only the formula prayers. For him, the formula prayers are like the melody of a song , and he is unconscious of the "words", the meaning of the mystery of the decade.

When the rosary is prayed well, the mind is engaged by the mystery of the decade, while at the same time the formula prayers pulse through the meditation like music, introducing each mystery with the gospel completeness of the *Our Father*, and then bathing each mystery in the Marian dimension so important to the Catholic faith. The mystery is then summed up in a Glory Be, that is, in the glory of the ultimate and central mystery, the Holy Trinity. The repetitive praying of the ten Hail Marys gives to each of the mysteries of the rosary the fully human foundation that Mary brings to the whole incarnation. From her completely human flesh, the humanity of Christ was formed. Because of Mary, and through her, Jesus was Son of Man. The role of Mary, and the great honor due her, is formed in the Christian in the beautiful prayer, the rosary. At the same time, the mysteries of salvation are meditated upon, and begin to enlighten the mind and heart with the saving truths of the faith.

It is essential to the Christian growing in the interior life, to grow in Christ - to grow in knowing Him, and loving Him, and serving Him. Scripture, and the holy mysteries of the faith we find therein, is His Self-revealing Word, the foundation for all we know of Him. As St. Jerome said, "Ignorance of the Scriptures is ignorance of Christ."[67] Our mediation must be grounded in the Word. There are many ways we can "pray Scripture" - we have in the Church many schools and methods, including the simple and common prayer of the rosary. We must grow close to Christ through His Word, and for every step we take toward Him in prayer, He takes ten or a hundred toward us! He is, indeed, much closer than we can know, even in this second station of the great saving work within us.

Examination of Conscience in the Second Station

I pray to be led not into temptation: do I walk by myself into situations of temptation? Do I resist the grace of God that would help me against sin, and thereby welcome my own weakness in temptation? Do I set myself up for the fall into sin? Following is an examination of conscience based on the three theological virtues of faith, hope and charity - first infused into the soul at Baptism.

1. *Faith*. I pray, "Our Father, who art in heaven, hallowed be thy name." Do I turn from the true revelation of God and His holy name, entrusted to the living Church? Do I prefer my

own ideas and speculations? Do I entertain false or partial teachings that contradict the authentic teachings of the Church, but that better serve my own self-interests? In the areas of our obligations to the poor, our use of money, and in the controversial issues of sexual morality such as contraception, divorce, homosexual and other extra-marital sexual acts, and abortion, do I open my heart to tempting lies?

2. *Hope*. I pray, "Thy kingdom come." Do I protect and treasure the hope set within me for God's justice and righteousness, for His holiness and peace? Do I open myself to any of the cynical and dark attitudes so prevalent in our society? Do I willingly listen to all the "bad news" around us, and believe in that above the "good news" of Jesus Christ? Am I cynical, despairing of real happiness or truth? Do I lead myself into temptation to despair, joining in the "bad news" complaints of common conversation?

Do I sin against hope not by despair but by presumption? Do I presume upon the love of God, and refuse to believe in His justice and righteousness, and in the abhorrence of sin in His sight? Do I lead myself into temptation to presumption, by refusing to truly know myself or to truly know God? Do I want Him not to change my own heart, but instead to love the sins that I love?

3. *Charity*. Do I lead myself into temptations to selfishness, to self-centeredness, to self-indulgence, to idolatries, to extreme individualism, to hedonism, to unbelief? All these contradict the simple definition of charity, which is the love of God because of who He is, and the love of neighbor because of God. Do I settle for a superficial knowledge of God and His love? I pray for "our daily bread," but do I refuse to look at the needs of the poor? I pray to "our Father," but do I mean no more than "my distant god"? Do I keep people distant from my heart, and so enable my own detachment from them? Do I look

upon persons as things, and value them only to the extent that they please me? Do I close my eyes to the image of God in others and in myself, and so harden my own heart to His love?

Prayer

Most Holy God, our Father,

You pour light into our hearts through Jesus Christ: you allow us to see and to struggle against the lures of temptation leading away from you. Through the power of your grace you guide us in the way of life and truth. Never abandon us, Holy Father, to the confusion within us – shepherd us, in the love of your Son.

The LORD is my shepherd, I shall not want;

he makes me lie down in green pastures.

He leads me beside still waters;

he restores my soul.

He leads me in paths of righteousness

for his name's sake.

Even though I walk through the valley of the

shadow of death,

I fear no evil;

for thou art with me;

thy rod and thy staff,

they comfort me.

Thou preparest a table before me

in the presence of my enemies;

thou anointest my head with oil,

my cup overflows.

Surely goodness and mercy shall follow me

all the days of my life;

and I shall dwell in the house of the LORD

for ever. (Psalm 23)

> *St. Ignatius of Loyola, you have helped the whole Church in the discernment of the heart: pray for us. Amen.*

Chapter 7. The Third Station: Forgive us our trespasses as we forgive those who trespass against us.

The Station of Mercy

The third station of the interior liturgy is the station of mercy. The prayer here is "Forgive us our trespasses as we forgive those who trespass against us." The sacramental grace here prayed for, and given, is the grace of Reconciliation. This station corresponds to that third mansion within the soul in the *Interior Castle*, seen by St. Teresa of Avila.[68]

In her picture of the third mansions of the interior castle, Teresa described souls who have made great progress in prayer. They are aware of the ugliness of evil and sin, eager to do works of charity, and temperate in their own ways of life. Teresa warns of the danger here, however, of a lack of right humility that must come by true self-knowledge. Souls here need to recognize and learn from their own faults, and not focus so on the faults of others. For such a soul, then, the third station of the interior liturgy has been entered. The appropriate prayer of this soul, in this station, becomes the petition, "Forgive us our trespasses, as we forgive those who trespass against us."

The station of mercy has a singular importance, among the seven important stations of the interior liturgy. This is the last of the ascetical stations, and the final place of preparation for a new and mystical work of God. Here we will find a bridge, therefore, but also a barrier. This station is one of unique consequence: will we receive all the graces awaiting us here, to enable His liturgy to continue, or will we instead find only a task that we cannot and will not meet? There is a fundamental choice and possibility here! Mercy was first given to us in the grace to believe, to be baptized and to begin the saving liturgy in Christ. A new share of mercy is offered to us here in the third station of the interior liturgy: for us to continue in His mercy, as we learn in this station, we must be open to give His mercy. We must receive in this station the grace and the willingness to give.

As the second station before it, so also the third station of the interior liturgy is a move toward deeper interiority. The first station was the initial confrontation with evil, and with the finding of deliverance in Christ. The second station was the engagement of the soul in the struggle with evil within: the struggle with our desires and temptations to cooperate with evil. In this third station, we begin to see more deeply our culpability in our own sin, and our part in the hardness of this whole world of sin. This third station is an encounter of the soul with the limitless mercy of God that is, by His will, limited by the openness of the human heart. The boundless and divine mercy that is infinite in scope and depth, a mercy that will forgive all sin, by the divine will cannot penetrate a heart hardened against the forgiveness of others. Jesus said,

> "Therefore the kingdom of heaven may be compared to a king who wished to settle accounts with his servants. When he began the reckoning, one was brought to him who owed him ten thousand talents; and as he could not pay, his lord ordered him to be sold, with his wife and children and all that he had, and payment to be made. So the servant fell on his knees, imploring him, 'Lord, have patience with me, and I will pay you everything.' And out of pity for him the lord of that servant released him and forgave him the debt.

> But that same servant, as he went out, came upon one of his fellow servants who owed him a hundred denarii; and seizing him by the throat he said, 'Pay what you owe.' So his fellow servant fell down and besought him, 'Have patience with me, and I will pay you.' He refused and went and put him in prison till he should pay the debt.

> When his fellow servants saw what had taken place, they were greatly distressed, and they went and reported to their lord all that had taken place.

Then his lord summoned him and said to him, 'You wicked servant! I forgave you all that debt because you besought me; and should not you have had mercy on your fellow servant, as I had mercy on you?' And in anger his lord delivered him to the jailers, till he should pay all his debt.

So also my heavenly Father will do to every one of you, if you do not forgive your brother from your heart."[69]

"Should you not have had mercy on your fellow servant?" The answer is to be yes: we ought to have mercy. God wants us to be a people of mercy, because mercy is true. God is merciful - our life depends upon His mercy - and He has created us in the divine image: to be true to Him and to ourselves, we must be merciful. To say it another way, to stand outside of mercy - to stand apart from the receiving and the giving of mercy - we deny our own nature and vocation to communion of life in Him.

In the petition of this station, we pray for the mercy of God, for the forgiveness of our transgression against Him. Yet this petition is not as simple as one that we might write; God has placed a "daunting" condition into our prayer. The need of human hearts is not only to receive mercy from God, but we need as well to be merciful toward others. Mercy must be given, if it is to be also received. God is rich in mercy! Yet the *Catechism* writes, in describing the abundantly offered mercy of God,

> Now - and this is daunting - this outpouring of mercy cannot penetrate our hearts as long as we have not forgiven those who have trespassed against us. Love, like the Body of Christ, is indivisible; we cannot love the God we cannot see if we do not love the brother or sister we do see. [Cf. 1 Jn 4:20] In refusing to forgive our brothers and sisters, our hearts are closed and their hardness makes them impervious to the Father's merciful love; but in confessing our sins, our hearts are opened to his grace.[70]

In our meditation upon this petition of the prayer, we

must include the strong counsel of the *Catechism*. We read here of hearts that even divine mercy "cannot penetrate" because "we have not forgiven those who have trespassed against us." Such human hearts are closed against God! We may try to justify our unrelenting hardness against some one or ones who badly hurt us. Perhaps they hurt someone close to us, beloved by us - perhaps someone innocent, and vulnerable, perhaps a child, or an elderly and weak person.

We may have good reason to be angry, and to proclaim that we can never and will never forget or forgive this hurt! Then how can we pray the *Our Father*? How can we say this petition, "forgive us as we forgive those..."? How can we read this hard word in the *Catechism* that judges us, in our judgement against that other? How can we reconcile this teaching, "In refusing to forgive our brothers and sisters, our hearts are closed and their hardness makes them impervious to the Father's merciful love...."

The *Catechism* points us to the answer, "...but in confessing our sins, our hearts are opened to his grace." Only His grace - this generous and undeserved share in His very life and love - can work the miracle, the supernatural good, of forgiveness. Through grace we receive His forgiveness for our many, many sins. In His grace we are able to do what outside of Him we cannot do: we can love with His love, and forgive with His forgiveness.

The meaning of forgiveness

We must be clear about forgiveness, what it is and what it is not. Forgiveness is not declaring the wrong act right. It does not erase the transgression, or pretend that it never happened, or that it is now acceptable. If it was wrong then, it is wrong now. If it was a sin, it is a sin. If I was violated, or hurt, or abused, or transgressed in any way, then the wrong stands as wrong - a transgression against me, or someone I love, and against God. To forgive the person who trespassed against me is not to accept the wrong as now somehow right.

To forgive a person is, however, to let go of any desire for vengeance. "Beloved, never avenge yourselves, but leave it to the wrath of God; for it is written, 'Vengeance is mine, I will repay, says the Lord.'" (Rom 12:19) To forgive is first of all to trust God as just. God will judge all persons: His justice is good and His judgment is perfect. We have, every one of us, been abused and hurt by people - some more cruelly and more deeply than others, of course. In this world darkened by sin, we all have been wounded, and we all have hurt and misused others! If every person sought to repay his own hurts, there would be no one left standing.

To forgive is secondly, and perhaps more importantly, to be on God's side in love for that person who hurt us. To forgive is fundamentally to give - to pass on, in fact, what we have first received: the love of God in Christ Jesus. To forgive the person who hurt us is to trust God first to rightly judge that other person, whom we cannot judge because we do not know his heart. To forgive is most deeply, however, to want good for that person and not evil. To forgive is to love, indeed to love with divine charity given us with grace in Baptism. God so loved the whole world, that He sent His only Son.... (Jn 3:16)

This petition of the *Our Father*, and this station of the interior liturgy, carries us to a deep void in the darkness within ourselves. We encounter through this petition a place in the heart of hollow emptiness, that cries out in fear for life and love, and instinctively, so to speak, strikes out in self-defense toward anyone who would threaten us. This void is made to be filled - filled to overflowing with God and His love. In this station we choose: is it to be the way we knew before we received this great grace of Christ, or is it to be the new way, the Gospel way, the way of life?

The work of Christ in the soul in this station of the liturgy is so far the most interior penetration into the very heart and _self_ of the person. The first station revealed the presence of evil threatening the person; the second, the temptation to cooperate with that evil even within his own soul. Here, in the third station, God shows us more than the presence of darkness - He begins to show us that this darkness is empty of what is essential to good and even to life itself. This revelation of emptiness is not fully complete, in this station - only later do we understand all that these words mean - but we are shown here the absolute demand on God's part: to be forgiven, we must forgive. To continue in His loving forgiveness for ourselves, we must share His forgiving love for others.

<u>Charity in the third station</u>

We begin to see a spiritual imperative in this station of Christ's interior work, and the crucial importance that it has! We need God's mercy; we must become persons of mercy. This station is the encounter of the soul with charity, and therefore, with spiritual life itself. The first station of the interior liturgy was deliverance from the evil that is death. The second station brought struggles yet victory in the temptations that lead to death. Here in the third station, positively, is the encounter with the challenge to live.

This station touches upon love itself - or more precisely, charity - that is life. Charity is infused into the soul at Baptism, yet in seed form. The *Catechism* defines charity: "Charity is the theological virtue by which we love God above all things for his own sake, and our neighbor as ourselves for the love of God."[71] In the English language, "love" is a very vague word: we can "love" some particular food, we can "love" some given sport, we can "love" a spouse, we can "love" God. Charity is more precise. Charity is that divine love grounded and founded upon God, given meaning by God who is love. Charity, simply stated, is love for God because of who He is, and love for others because of God.

It is this "because of" that separates charity from lesser loves. It is the motive, the desire of the heart that makes charity what it is, separate from "mere" love. We can love selfishly, but charity does not have room for selfishness. Mere "love" can be directed to saving oneself in the world; charity welcomes the out-pouring of self, the losing of oneself in this world in order to save it for the next. (CF Lk 9:24)

It is impossible to overstate the value of charity to the human soul. Charity is life. Apart from charity, the soul lies dead before God. Charity is the goal of the entire spiritual journey; the purpose of human life. The Catechism summarizes:

> "If I . . . have not charity," says the Apostle, "I am nothing." Whatever my privilege, service, or even virtue, "if I . . . have not charity, I gain nothing." [1 Cor 13:1-4] Charity is superior to all the virtues. It is the first of the theological virtues: "So faith, hope, charity abide, these three. But the greatest of these is charity." [1 Cor 13:13]

> The practice of all the virtues is animated and inspired by charity, which "binds everything together in perfect harmony" [Col 3:14]; it is the form of the virtues; it articulates and orders them among themselves; it is the source and the goal of their Christian practice. Charity upholds and purifies our human ability to love, and raises it to the supernatural perfection of divine love.

> The practice of the moral life animated by charity gives to the Christian the spiritual freedom of the children of God. He no longer stands before God as a slave, in servile fear, or as a mercenary looking for wages, but as a son responding to the love of him who "first loved us" [Cf. 1 Jn 4:19]:

> If we turn away from evil out of fear of punishment, we are in the position of slaves. If we pursue the enticement of wages, . . . we resemble mercenaries. Finally if we obey for the sake of

the good itself and out of love for him who commands . . .
we are in the position of children. [St. Basil]

... Love is itself the fulfillment of all our works. There is the
goal; that is why we run: we run toward it, and once we reach
it, in it we shall find rest. [St. Augustine] [72]

The place of decision

All that has been considered so far in this third station
helps us to see the unique and decisive place it has in the interior liturgy. The third station brings a crucial encounter with
charity, and the perhaps fearful possibilities of really embracing
it. To continue with the Lord in this work is to let go of the
hardness of my heart! It is to risk my vulnerabilities and weaknesses and really trust Him with my life! To forgive those who
have trespassed against me is to open myself to His love in a
way that threatens me in the deepest places of my heart.

The outcome of this encounter with the meaning of forgiveness is not certain. God gives us a freedom as persons to say
"yes" or to say "no" to this radical new possibility of faith. The
petition of the *Our Father* in this station can be a door into a
wholly new relationship with Him in Christ, or it can be an
impenetrable barrier through which we will not pass. Many
will not risk the "yes" God wants to hear. Those who fail to
pray this prayer in faith, in the grace that God offers, stop the
liturgy here perhaps for many years, perhaps for the rest of
their lives. The liturgy cannot continue in the soul of a human
person without passing through this station! The *Catechism*
insists, "In refusing to forgive our brothers and sisters, our
hearts are closed and their hardness makes them impervious to
the Father's merciful love." Cut off from the Father's love, we
stagnate; we die.

As the *Catechism* helps us to see, hope is available to us,
enabling us to continue in the liturgy, even though we might
feel paralyzed in an impossible demand to forgive. The soul can

indeed be paralyzed at this challenge to forgive, yet we are encouraged: "in confessing our sins, our hearts are opened to his grace." The Lord understands well our weak faith, our trembling hearts. He does not require the impossible of us. He makes the impossible possible, through the transforming potency of His empowering grace. What is required of us, in our fears, is faith. We must believe that His word is true: our hardness is wrong; our refusal to forgive is wrong. My refusal to love the brother who has trespassed against me is a sin - my sin, my sin against him and against God.

I must confront the fear in my heart with the hope of faith. I must believe His truth, even the truth that judges me. I must confess my hardness as the sin that it is, and I must seek His forgiveness. This confession, in humility and in faith, draws from the infinite mercy of God His enabling grace and love. In confessing my sin, my heart is opened once more to His grace, and I can begin again. With His grace, I can love even my enemies. With His grace, I can live even His life.

Reconciliation - the Sacrament of the Third Station

The sacrament that specifically illuminates this station, revealing its meaning, is the sacrament of Reconciliation. This seems obvious, because we pray for forgiveness in this petition. We pray in fact for more than merely legal or juridical forgiveness from God for our transgressions - we want, we need true reconciliation with Him, true restoration of loving relationship. The sacrament of Confession, or Reconciliation, brings this very grace and hence is the sacramental type and means for the prayer of this station.

We pray also for the grace to forgive, as well as the grace of forgiveness. Grace is a participation in the life of God! Grace is that which enables man, the divine image, to live in a human way the divine life. Grace enables us to do what we cannot do otherwise: we are enabled to be reconciled to God, and to live in peace and reconciliation with our neighbors.

Reconciliation and preparation for the altar

The entire Liturgy of the Word, in the communal celebration of the Mass, prepares the gathered people for the altar of sacrifice, and the communion that follows. So also in the interior liturgy, the liturgy of the Word, which includes these first three stations, is ordered to reconciliation with God and preparation for the second movement: the consecration at the altar. The fourth station of the interior liturgy, to which this present one looks forward and anticipates, is the consecration at the interior altar, celebrated with the petition, "Give us this day our daily bread." It is fitting that this present station calls us to reconciliation; it is fitting that this present prayer cries out, "Forgive us our trespasses...."

This station is a crucially important one to the soul. As has been said, it is a passageway opening to a wholly new relationship with God in Christ, or it is a wall, a barrier, a dead end. If the person will not open his heart to the true nature of mercy, then he will stand facing an impenetrable wall beyond which the liturgy cannot proceed. True human mercy is a participation in the life and love of God, and this mercy must flow both ways from a free and open heart. Freely have we received, freely are we to give. If we succeed in this station, and welcome the saving work of Christ unique to this place in our discipleship, then we will enter a most beautiful dimension of human life in Christ: human solidarity and communion. This dimension is finally prepared for, here in this station.

Prayer in the Third Station

The third station of the interior liturgy works the grace of community, and brings the final development of ascetical prayer, the prayer of simplicity. Prayer in the third station becomes a prayer of rest and waiting, so to speak as on a bridge to the other side, waiting for the radically new prayer communion of the soul called mystical prayer. The prayer of simplicity is a restful awaiting, a quietness in the presence of the Lord, a stillness as with a friend. The friend is Christ the Son of God - yet the friend is also every person, and any person.

Grace for community and solidarity

An immediate grace in this station is the grace of reconciliation, empowering and enabling us into the deeper communion that this prayer is working. The interior liturgy is a work of love, bringing forth both the giving and the receiving of love. This love must reach to embrace God, and neighbor. This love must welcome the community of persons. We pray "our" Father, we pray for the forgiving, the giving, the leading not, the delivering of "us." Here, in this station of mercy, our hearts are offered to genuine love for the community. Here, we offer our hearts to the work of the theological virtue infused at Baptism, charity. Here, we open our hearts to the "us" of our prayer.

Can we not see the absolute necessity of this work? If so, we can understand the mysterious and the beautiful gift of this petition, and this station. Jesus reinforces the necessity of this work, after giving the prayer: "For if you forgive men their trespasses, your heavenly Father also will forgive you; but if you do not forgive men their trespasses, neither will your Father forgive your trespasses." (Mt 6:14-15) Jesus did not immediately expound on any other petition of His prayer - but this one He did, underlining the crucial importance of it. We cannot remain alone, isolated, individualistic. We are persons, made in the image of God, made for communion in love!

Our communion with God is inseparable from our communion with other human persons. The walls that keep us from God have bricks with human names. Even our communication with Him in prayer is contingent upon our openness to our brothers and sisters: "And whenever you stand praying, forgive, if you have anything against any one; so that your Father also who is in heaven may forgive you your trespasses." (Mk 11:25)

The grace of reconciliation enables us to pray in genuineness of heart for others. This petition begins to form us in the virtue of charity, and prepares us for the continuing work ahead.

The prayer of simplicity

In the third station, prayer develops from meditation into the prayer of simplicity. As we grow in inner knowing of the Lord, through meditation on His sacred Self-revelation, our communion in peace with Him grows. Through knowledge of Him and His truth - and more, through the actual living of all that we know of His truth - then the soul becomes more quiet in His presence, more able to simply sit with Him.

There is no real "short-cut" to this prayer! Some teachers of prayer would have us try to force entry into this rest with God by means of physical positioning, or special chants, or breathing techniques, or mental exercises. The prayer of simplicity is found as the proper fruit of the tree of meditation, planted firmly in the ground of vocal prayer. We never leave or "outgrow" vocal prayer - indeed the sacred liturgy of the Church is in a sense a "vocal prayer." Nor are we able to rest in peace in the presence of a God we have not bothered to come to know in meditation, or cared to obey. Neither can we expect simple quietness with Him, if we have declined His graced presence in the sacraments. The prayer of simplicity, in other words, is part of the interior liturgy of His saving work, requiring our part and cooperation in vocal prayer, in meditation upon truth, in a faithful moral life, and in an observant religious life in the sacraments.

" … as we forgive …": Prelude to the Darkness before Consecration

The second part of this petition, "as we forgive those who trespass against us," anticipates the second major movement of the interior liturgy, the consecration at the altar of the cross. This petition, in other words, anticipates and in a sense hastens the personal embrace of the cross. "As" is a bridge to the illuminative stage of the spiritual journey, and so is an anticipation of its prerequisite, the dark night of the senses. The person finds himself, in this station, on a bridge, and bridges allow movement both ways. He can go forward, or he can fall back. This is the first conditional "as", of the two in the prayer, that we have encountered thus far. The provisory, conditional nature of this petition, in the word "as", places us on the bridge with two possible outcomes: we can go on to the side of continuing forgiveness in Christ and growing life in Him, or we can fall back from Him, remaining in the hard refusal to forgive. If we proceed through this petition, which is the true desire of our hearts, we will face a great trial – the trial named by St. John of the Cross as the dark night of the senses. If we fall back, succumbing to the fears and isolation of a lower self, we will condemn ourselves to a great tragedy for any human person: we will fail to become ourselves, as true images of God.

The work of an interior purification that only God can do in the soul is awaiting us at this point, at this station in the liturgy. The bridge of this "as" carries me to a purging desert of barrenness, of emptiness and fruitlessness. Prayer becomes dry, even seeming to be only myself talking to myself. In the first

stations of the saving work, it seemed that Christ was so near!
My prayers were so often answered, His loving care was so
certain, His forgiveness so merciful, so generous! He gave me
strength to refuse the sins and temptations that were death to
me! But now, it all has changed. As the psalmist experienced:

> I cry aloud to God, aloud to God, that he may hear me.
>
> In the day of my trouble I seek the Lord; in the night my hand
> is stretched out without wearying; my soul refuses to be com-
> forted. I think of God, and I moan; I meditate, and my spirit
> faints. Thou dost hold my eyelids from closing; I am so trou-
> bled that I cannot speak.
>
> I consider the days of old, I remember the years long ago. I
> commune with my heart in the night; I meditate and search
> my spirit: "Will the Lord spurn for ever, and never again be
> favorable? Has his steadfast love for ever ceased? Are his prom-
> ises at an end for all time? Has God forgotten to be gracious?
> Has he in anger shut up his compassion?" And I say, "It is my
> grief that the right hand of the Most High has changed."
>
> I will call to mind the deeds of the LORD; yea, I will remem-
> ber thy wonders of old. I will meditate on all thy work, and
> muse on thy mighty deeds.
>
> Thy way, O God, is holy. What god is great like our God?[73]

The trials of this station - the dark night of the senses -
were experienced by the disciples of Jesus in the terrible time of
the passion: the arrest, the trial, the crucifixion, the death and
burial. In this time of darkness and trial, all that they knew of
Jesus seemed to vanish. Where was His power? Where was His
authority? Where was His place of privilege with God? Now,
He seemed powerless, and all their confidence, as disciples of
the great master, dissolved. This is a necessary dark night for
every disciple of Jesus! In the interior liturgy of Christ, this is
a necessary work in which we are called to a deeper self-aban-
donment and trust than we have ever yet known.

What is the dark night of the senses? The psalmist has
written well of it in the passage above. In a day of trouble that

may stretch into many days, he seeks the Lord without weary-
ing - yet where is He? He continues to look to God, yet his soul
finds no comfort. There is no consolation to be found anywhere - not in the things of God, nor in the things of the
world. He tries to meditate upon all he knows of God, but his
spirit faints. He cannot meditate as he used to, but instead seeks
to quietly look to Him without the efforts of deliberate discur-
sive meditation. He remembers the days of old, when God was
so near, so close, so available - but now, where is He? Has He
changed? Has He forgotten me? Has He abandoned me?

The way of faithfulness and perseverance are his only real
choices. He will call to mind His works of before, and he will
wait. He will trust. God is holy; He only is our God.

<u>The necessary dark night</u>

St. John of the Cross can help us to understand this trial,
but the darkness and dryness and the depth of hunger carved
out within us hardly seem any easier to endure. This is a time
for trust. Faith, hope and charity are being refined as in a fire -
and fires burn and bring to the surface many imperfections and
impurities that have been mixed within. The need is to trust
God in His saving work: to believe that He is indeed working
good; to wait, and hope, and persevere.

Reasons for the necessary purgations and purifications of
the first dark night are presented in more detail in the previous
work[74], and by other authors. In spite of our willingness, and
cooperation, and even zeal in our discipleship, there remain
defects in the soul so deep that only God can touch and heal
them. The three cardinal ones - spiritual pride, spiritual sen-
suality, and spiritual sloth - require a work that only God can
do. Our necessary part is to trust Him in the darkness that will
come upon us.

It may be that the first dark night has a purpose even more

fundamental than the necessary requirement because of our sins. We do need, because of our sin, the outside intervention, so to speak, of the hand of God. But we see a dark night in the life of Adam even before his fall into sin, when he was still in original innocence and grace. The Lord caused a "deep sleep to fall upon the man," in which the Lord formed his companion and spouse, Eve. (Gen 2:21) This can be seen as a foreshadowing of the cross, out of the darkness of which was formed the Church, the Bride of Christ. But in a smaller way, perhaps, we can see the working in darkness of the gift to Adam of communion, of the covenant of love. Before the deep sleep, in his naming of the animals, he could begin to realize the profound human solitude of his existence – but only in the deep sleep would God form the reality of communion for him.

We see also a dark night for sinless Mary, in the terrible days of separation from her Son in His twelfth year, in the trip to Jerusalem for the Passover. (Lk 2:41-52) She was without sin, yet there was for her here and would be again at the cross a night of darkness, of profound spiritual significance and meaning. She did not understand this troubling experience, nor the explanation of Jesus to her, yet she "kept all these things in her heart." (Lk 2:51) Mary shows us, in her example, that even without our personal sin there will be darkness and suffering for those who follow Christ. It was prophesied to her that "a sword will pierce through your own soul also," (Lk 2:35) and this will come for all in His Church: we are all given a cross to carry. We see, however, that this trial of darkness must not surprise us or cause dismay. There is sin within us that only God can deal with. And more, there is a work for communion that God chooses to work in darkness, in His mystery, in His love. Our part is to trust Him.

Communion requires mercy

Why does the Lord command us to pray in this strange

way - to link our needed forgiveness for our own trespasses, to our forgiveness of those who trespass against us? He does command what seems to be at first impossible - for in the beginning we cannot forgive! In the beginning of our discipleship, and our journey with Him, we cannot give what we do not have, and we do not have mercy for others in the measure required of us by God.

There is a hardness of heart common to man. We find this insensitivity and lack of refinement of heart in the disciples of Jesus. In the ministry of Jesus before the cross, and before the resurrection, Peter once asked Him, "Lord, how often shall my brother sin against me, and I forgive him? As many as seven times?" Jesus said to him, "I do not say to you seven times, but seventy times seven." (Mt 18:21-22) When our mercy has a limit, a boundary, then it is not the divine mercy and we are not able to offer as Church the mercy of God to the world. This mercy, even extended seven times, is not sufficient to show to the world the transforming power of Christ. This mercy, limited to seven times, is not the mercy Jesus came to give the world. It is not enough.

In the formation of the disciples of Jesus, we see the completeness of His liturgy not in His earthly ministry, not even immediately after the cross, but only after His ascension and the gift of the Holy Spirit at Pentecost. In the lives of His first disciples we do not see, in the time they were with Him before the cross, the heroic virtue to which they were called. In these first disciples we do not see the power of Christ in them even in that intermediate period between the cross and the ascension. It is only after the ascension and Pentecost, in the power of the Holy Spirit, that we see in those disciples the heroic sanctity that was their vocation from the beginning. At Pentecost, we see the love of God poured into human persons, in the Person of the Holy Spirit - poured even unto overflowing.

After Pentecost, we see the mercy of God abiding in human persons. After the gift of the Holy Spirit at Pentecost, we see the life of Jesus Christ alive in the Church. This is the completeness of the liturgy of Christ; this is His saving work made perfect. When the Church truly lives the life of Christ, she is who she most truly is called to be: the Body of Christ, His beloved spouse. In our human expression of His life, personally and ecclesially, the Church lives her vocation in this world.

We hear the mercy of God alive in human persons after Pentecost. We hear Stephen, the first Christian martyr, speaking words not possible except in living communion with Christ. As he was being stoned to death, he prayed for his killers, "Lord, do not hold this sin against them." (Acts 7:60) We hear James exhorting the Church to a living witness to this authentic divine wisdom: "But the wisdom from above is first pure, then peaceable, gentle, open to reason, full of mercy and good fruits, without uncertainty or insincerity." (James 3:17)

Why does the Lord point us, in this petition, to a mercy for others that we do not yet have, linking it to His mercy for ourselves that we so clearly need? Because our vocation, like the vocation of the first disciples of Jesus, is ordered toward fullness and perfection that is not yet accomplished. In praying this strange petition, we are asking for virtue we do not have, but that we must have if we are to ever fully be ourselves, and fully be Church. In this petition, we are asking God to do in us what we cannot do for ourselves; we are offering ourselves to Him in the darkness and obscurity of faith, saying in effect, "Lord, make me an instrument of your forgiveness; make me merciful."

Why then does the Lord command us to pray in this conditional way? Yes, He commands us to this petition! He forces us, so to speak, to face the obligation, as His disciple, to enter

His mercy in so full a way that we become participants - collaborators - in His outpouring of mercy upon the world. Jesus came to gather human persons into His saving work, His liturgy. Jesus came to gather and to send out a Church in His name. With this petition He binds mercy with justice so intimately that there is no escape from the one without the other! By commanding us to pray in this way, He forces us, so to speak, to open ourselves interiorly to the terrible and necessary work of God, called the dark night of the soul.

In this way, the third station of the interior liturgy places us on the threshold of a transformation we cannot anticipate, not even intelligently pray for. The simple "as we forgive" invites the Lord to penetrate the stony hearts we bring to Him, and to transform them from within. We cannot simply forgive each other, "as the Lord has forgiven you, so you also must forgive." (Col 3:13) We cannot simply, "Be merciful, even as your Father is merciful." (Lk 6:36) To possess the mercy we must have within our hearts, we cannot simply claim it or act it or try to force ourselves into it! We must ask and seek for this mercy, knocking at the door of the Source Himself. God Himself must transform our hearts anew. He must do in us the miracle He promised, "A new heart I will give you, and a new spirit I will put within you; and I will take out of your flesh the heart of stone and give you a heart of flesh." (Ez 36:26)

Examination of Conscience in the Third Station

If we allow it, the *Our Father*, as the God-given norm of our prayer, will probe our hearts for the mercy and the loving communion that we need. I pray "our" Father: do I see my brother, do I see my sister, in the person who is before me? Do I see His divine fatherhood within the strangers, the enemies, the poor, the little ones? Do I see Him in the face of the person I encounter at Mass, at the store, at school, at my dinner table?

I pray, "give us this day our daily bread." Do I see Him in the faceless suffering poor at my gates, like poor Lazarus at the gate of the rich man (Lk 16:20): in the millions of poor faceless little ones aborted, and poor faceless thousands in prison, and poor countless ones I do not know who are the hungry of the world?

I pray, "lead us not into temptation, but deliver us from evil." Do I know the solidarity we all possess in Christ, and therefore the debt I owe to every person to help him in his journey to holiness? Do I carefully guard the innocence of others, that I might never be a source of temptation for another? Is my speech, my dress, my conversation and my example ordered not toward temptation but toward the sanctification of others? Do I contribute in any way to the means of evil in the world, through its misuse of magazines, television, movies, music or theater?

Prayer

Most Holy Lord God, our Father – You call us to great light, and reveal a darkness within us. You call us to love, and show us a hardness in our hearts. You sent to us Jesus your Son, who opened the floodgates of mercy to stream forth without limit from His pierced and Sacred Heart. Out of His agony for sinners, dear Father, only mercy flows forth! Never let us harden ourselves against His life and love; never let us shut out His mercy. Give us the grace and freedom of forgiveness toward all men. St. Faustina, advocate of the divine mercy, pray for us. Amen.

Section 2. The Second Movement: the Liturgy of Consecration

The second great movement of Christ at work in the soul usually comes as a surprising and new and personal experience of Him, interiorly. Some describe this as being "born again", or as receiving a new and second conversion. As the work of the first movement was one of reformation, this work is one of transformation. This movement corresponds, in traditional Catholic spirituality, to the stage of the proficients, or the illuminative stage of the spiritual life.

Prayer and Mary in the Liturgy of Consecration

Here the person is given a precious gift: the prayer of infused contemplation. Here, the prayer communion with God in Christ becomes undeniably, experientially, dialogue. Here, there is no question in the soul concerning the presence, the nearness or the abiding love of God: He is with me, here and now, in prayer. Before, the nearness of God in prayer was a matter of faith believed. Now, this is a matter of the holy presence, experienced.

The second great movement of the interior liturgy initiates a radically new relationship with God in Christ. The difference between the first and the second movements in the interior liturgy is similar to the difference that occurs in the communal liturgy, in the Mass, when the priest moves from the liturgy of the Word over to the altar for the sacred consecration of the bread and the wine. This difference in the interior liturgy can be understood through the way in which the presence of Christ changes in the communal liturgy, from the first movement to the second. Jesus Christ is truly, really present in the communal liturgy in His holy Word, holy Scripture. But Jesus Christ is present in a radically new and different way, in our celebration of Holy Mass, upon the altar of consecration!

Within the soul, this difference is experienced in the interior liturgy upon entering the second great movement of the saving work of Christ. This is now the fourth station of the liturgy, the station of consecration at the altar of the heart. Prayer, in this station, is named the prayer of infused contemplation. It is the gift of the awareness of the holy presence in prayer.

<u>Mary in the liturgy of consecration</u>

The liturgy of consecration begins for us really in the dark night of the senses, at the foot of the cross. The prayer that initiates the dark night – that disquieting "as we forgive those who trespass against us" – in fact initiates the whole new work of God that is this new consecration to Him. Here standing near the cross, in the person of the beloved disciple, we find ourselves with Mary the mother of Jesus. Here, in the terrible glory of the crucifixion, we hear from Jesus a new responsibility, a new gift, a new closeness, a new bond begun: a new family.

Mary is given to us and received by us as mother: "Behold, your mother." (Jn 19:27) It is here that the light of the love of Christ, radiating from His complete self-gift in love, illuminates His mother. It is here that He reveals her, in a sense, to all His beloved disciples and here in His light she awaits us. It is here at His cross that we receive from Jesus what we could receive only here, and only from Him. Together, they all come and are all embraced in a new love and a new urgency: Mary, my brothers and sisters in Christ, my holy mother the Church, and the great apostolate awaiting us. All these are gathered into a single reality, given a mysterious unity by the glory of the light of the crucified One, that we only begin to understand but we will understand later.

We are invited - even urged from within - into an authentic Marian devotion in the liturgy of consecration. This new relationship in Christ with Mary is ordered toward a much deeper and more fully integrated Marian devotion in the final and third movement, the liturgy of communion. We will begin to understand, as we proceed and as His holy work in us proceeds, the true devotion to Mary as endorsed by the great saint, St. Louis de Montfort. Flowing so near to the living waters of His liturgy within us, is the prayerful maternal love of Mary! We begin to see, as His work progresses through the *Our Father*, the collaboration of Mary, His mother and ours. We begin to understand, with de Montfort, as we continue in the prayer, the journey to Jesus through Mary.

<u>The work of the apostolate</u>

Marian devotion begins to have new meaning in the liturgy of consecration. A deeply felt love for the Church is awakened, a personal relationship with Jesus Christ becomes real, and concern for the works and needs of the Church gains a personal importance. These all are gathered into the religious sense with a new urgency! All is seen in the real time of His suffering! All is seen also in the personal awareness of our own mortality, and the day of judgment awaiting us all. The imperatives of the Christian life, of the Church, now have a new emphasis and significance, laying upon each of us an insistent obligation that cannot be ignored. Through this work of consecration within the soul, the Church receives consecrated persons into her apostolate. Because of this new spiritual reality within, there is new zeal and fortitude expressed in Christian works. The whole Church is blessed, through the interior and personal blessing of this liturgy.

Prayer and work are seen, here, in a unity that was not understood before. All the new lights that awaken in this work of the interior liturgy are here only beginning, only starting -

and all these will find an ever greater intensity and clarity in the final work of the liturgy of communion. Yet now, the discoveries, the urgent imperatives, the call for zeal and personal response that are all heard within the soul are like a new birth, a new conversion, a new life in Christ. He calls us to an integrity that will ignore no part of our life! He calls us to a holiness that must be answered! He calls us to follow Him, in intimate prayer and in holy works, with an insistence that seems now permanently engraved upon our hearts. He calls, and we must answer.

Chapter 8. The Fourth Station: Give us this day our daily bread.

The Station of Consecration at the Altar

The fourth station of the interior liturgy is the station of consecration at the altar of the heart. The prayer here is, "Give us this day our daily bread ." The sacramental grace here prayed for, and given, is the grace of Holy Eucharist. This station corresponds to that fourth mansion within the soul in the *Interior Castle*, seen by St. Teresa of Avila.[75]

In her writings about the fourth mansions of the interior castle, Teresa described a great and radical advance in prayer, from ascetical into that prayer of infused contemplation rightly called mystical. The infused contemplation here entered is called the prayer of quiet. This prayer and relationship with Christ, Teresa described as spiritual delight, expanding the heart and enabling Christian love. The need of the soul here, concerning which Teresa cautioned, is the need to remain close to the Lord in prayer, returning quickly when anyone finds himself apart for some reason. One must stay close to the food of life and goodness, as a suckling child must stay close to the mother's breast. Here then, the work of Christ has entered the fourth station of the interior liturgy. Here, the soul prays the petition of the fourth station, "Give us this day our daily bread."

This petition stands at the very center of the *Our Father*. It is pivotal and central, in the flow of divine grace and human response, the receiving and giving in prayer-communion which is the *Our Father*. This particular petition stands in several senses as the heart and the summit of the prayer, corresponding as it does to the Eucharistic prayer in the liturgy of Holy Mass. The "heart and summit" of the celebration of the Mass comes with the *anaphora*, the Eucharistic prayer – and the prayer of *epiclesis* (see Addendum p. 224) in the communal liturgy is folded within this heart and summit.[76] To understand the place of this petition in the interior liturgy, and in the *Our Father*, we must understand the place of the epiclesis in the liturgy of the Church. This petition, in which we call out to God from our poverty, our loneliness, our hunger and our need, is indeed the epiclesis of the interior liturgy.

Several important centers come together for the Christian in this petition. First, this petition is the central fourth of the seven petitions of the *Our Father*: three petitions precede it and three petitions follow it. The three petitions that precede it look forward to this meeting at the table; they anticipate and stir a growing hunger for heavenly bread that is sought here. The three petitions that follow are all enabled and empowered by this bread, this grace, this encounter in Christ. The three petitions that precede are the petitions of asceticism, of ascetical prayer; the three that follow are the petitions of mysticism, of mystical prayer. At the very center of the prayer and of the life of prayer is this petition, "Give us this day our daily bread." Other senses of the crucial and central nature of this petition will be developed in this section.

The singular center of the liturgy

This petition for the saving and empowering bread from heaven stands in the very middle of the seven stations of the interior liturgy. Three petitions and stations precede it; three follow it. Most importantly, however, it follows the three stations of ascetical movement of the great interior work of salvation, and stands at the beginning of the mystical movement. The petition for the daily bread from heaven is the prayer of initiation into the mystical life, uttered at the interior altar of self-offering, illuminated and bathed in the divine light of the cross of Christ.

This petition is prayed not in the shadow of the cross but in its light. Before this station in the interior liturgy – before the soul has actually progressed to this plateau of the journey in Christ – the cross was indeed seen and understood as a shadow, a suffering of Christ to be acknowledged and received somehow in the obscurity of faith. As the first disciples of Jesus could not understand the prophesies of His cross and death and resurrection, so the Christian does not and cannot see the glory of the cross until this time, the new day, this crucial station in the interior liturgy.

The cross is the very center of human history. Human history, and the meaning of every human life after that momentous intervention of God in His creation, is forever now illuminated by the glory of Christ and His cross. All that came before the cross is understood as pre-Christian; all that has come afterward must be judged in the light of His Self-gift, so deeply permeated with divine mystery yet so humanly experienced in His own flesh and blood. The saving bread from heaven was given to us all only through His death on the cross. The meaning of His cross, in the interior liturgy of the Christian before this station, had been as Gift to be trusted and accepted and received. Now all is seen differently, as if for the first time, newly illuminated as if from within. Within the cross a light is perceived; from within the Sacred Heart of Jesus hanging there and dying, is a glory radiating and burning and enlightening the meaning of every human life.

The altar is the center of every church. This petition, "Give us this day our daily bread," is prayed from the altar of the heart, the very center of the human person. In the interior liturgy, this petition is the epiclesis offered up to the One who alone can fill the emptiness and hunger of the soul. In the liturgy of the Church, the altar is the place of consecration where the bread and wine become, through divine response to the prayer of epiclesis of the priest, the saving and Holy Eucharist. In the interior liturgy similarly, through the prayer of the heart-priest, the heavenly bread does come in a spiritual sense. This is the petition of epiclesis, the prayer of consecration offered at an interior altar, a mystical exchange bringing forth a spiritual Eucharist. Just as the altar is the center of the church and the place of consecration of all material gifts and therefore also the place of the prayer of epiclesis, so too here in this petition and at this station we stand in prayer at that interior altar of offering and sacrifice.

The petition, "Give us this day our daily bread," is prayed from the center of the truth of the human person. For this reason, the petition calls forward the interior vocation of heart-priest. This petition and this station of the interior liturgy begin the great flow of grace and power that unfold, so to speak, the call to the common priesthood in Christ that began in seed form on the day of our Baptism. It is our priesthood in Christ that offers the self-gift Paul spoke of, "Present your bodies a living sacrifice...." (Rom 12:1)

Our meaning as individual human persons is opened to us only through the nourishment of this divine bread which brings His life. It is through the divine bread that the mystery of the divine image, that image which is the defining mark of human nature, begins to unfold. The meaning of each human life is explained, or in a sense declared, more fully in the station that follows this one: the embrace of His will, done on earth as it is in heaven. But that holy and true will is done only through the empowering nourishment of Christ, in the bread come down from heaven. Human life makes sense only as we live the life of God - as we humanly express the divine image! The meaning of my life, or your life, becomes clear only in the light of the cross! The hunger of the human heart is satisfied finally, only with the bread come down from heaven, such that a man may eat of it and not die.

Eucharist – the Sacrament of the Fourth Station

The sacrament, of the seven sacraments, that specifically illuminates this station and its meaning, is the sacrament of Holy Eucharist. "Give us this day our daily bread" is the crucially important center of the *Our Father* and of the interior liturgy it guides. As the center of the liturgy, it begins the second major movement of God's saving work in the soul: the dawn of the mystical life with the great transforming gift of infused contemplation in prayer. Here is called forth the personal response to this gift of God – the self-offering of consecration – in a sense of second conversion, renewed zeal, and joy.

The ultimate and complete meaning of this petition is found in the Eucharist, the supernatural bread from heaven. Before we focus on the final meaning of this petition, we must listen to the intermediate meanings as well. This petition invites us to look to God our Father for our material bread, and by extension for all our legitimate material needs. There is nothing wrong with asking God to help us in the many needs we have as human persons – for food to sustain us, for clothes to cover us, for covering to shelter our vulnerable bodies from the extremes of heat and cold and wind and rain. Not only is there nothing wrong in so praying to God: we are told in this petition to pray in this way.

There are extremes to be avoided, in praying for our material needs. One extreme is to so over-spiritualize prayer, that we believe that any concern with material needs is unworthy. Certainly this is not our faith. The *Catechism* assures us that it is here, through this petition, that God offers us His loving concern for all our legitimate physical and material needs.

The other extreme is to over-materialize our prayer, and to remain in the immature relationship with God that sees in Him no more than our benefactor and provider in this life. We are made for more than this life! We must understand that this life is a gift to us, with all its trials and burdens as well as its joys and consolations, but this gift is a brief one, and it is only the beginning of an eternity. This petition for our daily bread does include our legitimate material needs, but it is heard in its fullness as it directs us to the bread from heaven, the Holy Eucharist.

The hunger for God

For what do I hunger? An important part of our interior journey to holiness and life in Christ is the change, the development, in our hunger. The journey begins with a hunger for life, yet poorly discerned. In the beginning of the interior liturgy, there is awakened in us a hunger, a desire for life - life against the death and the evil around us. Our prayer is, "deliver us from evil." Our hunger for God and the things of God, however, is very mixed and confused in hungers for the world and the things of the world.

We grow; we continue in our liturgy, and we pray for help in the temptations that are so close. These temptations are so close, and are such a danger, because true hunger is so poorly discerned. What bread do we need for this day? What bread do we really need? What will bring me happiness, and satisfaction? Our desires, and our prayers, are mixed. We work for two breads to satisfy two hungers, and we cannot see clearly enough the conflict of this mixture of hungers.

This station of the interior liturgy, however, is the great bridge between the world and heaven - it is the bridge of the cross, and the giving by Christ of the only bread that does satisfy the human soul. Christ exhorts us, "Do not labor for the food which perishes, but for the food which endures to eternal life." (Jn 6:27) How much of our effort is for that which does not last? How much striving is for the wind; how much grasping for sand only to spill from between our fingers? How much concern is for the trivial, and laboring for mere toys and coverings? Christ offers bread from heaven, that endures unto eternal life!

Here, in this central and crucial bridge of the great interior liturgy, our prayer looks to the very source of the life we were created for, and for which we hunger. The bread most essential and most necessary to us is God, God only, God our Source and our sustenance.

In this station of the interior liturgy, entering as we do into a new and precious communion with God in prayer – the prayer of infused contemplation – we are allowed a new and life-changing closeness to Him, and with Him. As this prayer grows and deepens, and pervades the entire soul, our communion indeed deepens to most precious communion in Him, and He in us. Here, in the fourth station of the interior liturgy, we are allowed to invite Him into our souls. He who became bread for us, orders us here to request, and take, and eat.

Bread of eternal life

Christian life began at the beginning of our liturgy, but the fullness of Christian living awaits us here and beyond this bridge – wholehearted self-gift to the apostolate, with true Sabbath rest upon the breast of Christ in contemplative prayer. At this station, here at the table of the Lord, is the divine food that alone can enable life to be fully Christian. The food is Christ Himself, as the Christian life is Christ the Son Himself.

It is through the bread come down from heaven, that we live. It is through this bread that we come into living relationship with God – a communion in God, for which human per-

sons are created. We can begin to understand this vitally important communion through the teaching of Jesus in the "Bread of
Life" discourse in John's Gospel. Jesus said, "As the living
Father sent me, and I live because of the Father, so he who eats
me will live because of me." (Jn 6:56-57)

In this passage, Jesus invites us to understand the mystery
of our communion with God, a mystery rooted in the interior
life of God Himself. The two truths are parallel: the Son lives
because of the Father; he who eats the Son will live because of
Him. Our life in Christ is explained through the great mystery
of the interior life of God the Holy Trinity. The Son, eternally
begotten by the Father, is eternally receiving His life, His divinity, His Being as God the Son, from God the Father. Here is an
aspect of that divine and eternal inferno of life, the Holy
Trinity, that directly explains our life as human persons created
in the image of God the Holy Trinity: our life flows from God
the Son. If we are to have life, we receive it from God the Son.
As the Son lives because of the Father, eternally receiving His
very Being from the Father, so we who hunger for life have our
Source as well.

His disciples could not understand at first, the mysterious
Source of the life of Jesus. He had bread to eat that they knew
not of! They could not understand His words, that as His life
is from the Father, so also our life is from Him and through
Him. This is the dialogue of life, and the dialogue of love, a
dynamic interchange that we must enter if we would live.

Christ has given Himself as Bread for the life of the world:
if we eat His flesh and drink His blood, He who is the only-
begotten of the Father will give this life to us. Indeed He is and
will be in us, this life for us. He is the door, the gate, the way
to the Father who is the Source and origin of all, and through
Him and only through Him can we live. He invites us into
Himself, even as He is in the Father! In Him, through this most

intimate communion as bread, we enter our vocation into God the Holy Trinity. In Him, in the bread come down out of heaven, the divine image at the root of our humanity finds its foundation. Thus we pray this most fundamental prayer, this bridge into the interior life of life itself, "Give us this day our daily bread."

Epiclesis

"Give us this day our daily bread" is the epiclesis of the interior liturgy. This petition of the *Our Father* is the inner resonance of the epiclesis of the communal liturgy, but now uttered interiorly at the altar of the heart. This petition, a prayer finally and ultimately from our need for the saving bread from heaven, brings us to the altar within - the personal cross - and to the table of mystical communion in Christ. The interior altar of the heart is that sacred center of the human person, made and held in reserve for God alone. It is forever empty until He is present upon it. The heart is forever alone, in an aloneness that is not good, until He comes to it.

The epiclesis is the cry of the poor in spirit, of those who hunger and thirst for righteousness. It is the cry of those who know the emptiness of all things and even of life itself, if not filled with the Spirit of God. In the epiclesis of the Mass, the Church asks the Father to send His Holy Spirit upon the gifts of bread and wine, so that they might become the body and blood of Jesus Christ. The epiclesis further asks God to enable, through His Spirit, that unity in Christ that is essential to humanity made in the divine image. The epiclesis acknowledges our humble dependency, yet looks to God in the confidence and magnanimity of faith. It is prayer for the life that only God can bring to the soul of His humble creature.

At the epiclesis all must wait in silence for the One who answers with Presence. At the epiclesis in the communal liturgy of the Church, we shut our mouths in reverence before God and wait for His powerful hand. In the Mass, we await the great gift. Our humble offerings, placed upon the altar, will become the body, blood, soul and divinity of Christ. So also at this epiclesis of the interior liturgy, there is a silent awaiting in darkness and unknowing, yet in faith. We prepare to open our hearts to His life in prayer. We have done all we can do; we have gathered our humble self-offerings before the Lord, placed them upon the interior altar of the heart, and we wait. We have, in our poor and incomplete way, presented our bodies a living sacrifice - yet we can only present, laying it upon the altar, and wait. Now, God alone can act.

Mary and the epiclesis

There is no greater or more complete example of the prayer of epiclesis than Mary. The epiclesis of Mary - her self-offering, her patient waiting for the omnipotent God - exceeds in purity and clarity the epiclesis of any priest on earth! Mary offered herself a living sacrifice with an integrity we cannot duplicate! In the unfathomable mercy of God, nevertheless, at every epiclesis at every altar of His holy Church, the priest offers our sacrifice with an efficacy that matches that of Mary! Christ Jesus comes to us, in our emptiness and openness, as He came to her! God gives us our daily bread, the holy Eucharist, in every Mass of His Church.

The epiclesis of Mary stands as a guiding beacon for our own prayer, as we pray in the liturgy within our souls: "Behold, I am the handmaid of the Lord; let it be to me according to your word." (Lk 1:38) Here is her self-offering - more than symbolic gifts of bread and wine, she offers immediately herself. Her own flesh and blood, the works of her body most intimately, the labors of the lifetime before her - all are placed upon the altar for the Lord. She withholds nothing, she offers her all. Mary, because of who she is, because of who God formed her to become, is worthy to hold the infinite treasure to be given. Mary immaculate opens her self in wholeness to the Lord, and waits.

God is pleased with her invitation, so simple and so pure. Without the duplicity that plagues us in our prayer, having no hidden self-serving motives, no mercenary incentives, no hidden agendas, Mary offers her simple "yes" to the will of God. God, who longs to gather us into His life and love, will respond: "The Holy Spirit will come upon you, and the power of the Most High will overshadow you...." (Lk 1:35) For Mary, following this epiclesis and the unprecedented work of God in her, there is coming a wholly new relationship with God in the Son, and through the Holy Spirit.

This stage of the saving work of Christ in us, in our interior liturgy, unveils God for us also, as for Mary, in a life-transforming way. God is known anew: Father, Son, and Holy Spirit. Christ Jesus becomes personal for us, as in a different but analogous way He became personal for Mary! The Holy Spirit becomes real for us, an experienced power for us, as in a different but analogous way His power was personally experienced in Mary! He reveals Jesus, as Jesus promised: "When the Spirit of truth comes, he will guide you into all the truth; ... He will glorify me, for he will take what is mine and declare it to you." (Jn 16: 13-14)

The necessary food for the journey

The bread from heaven is necessary for Christian life on earth. This is the substance of the Christian life, because it is the substance of Christ Himself. The Eucharist is the Christ, whole and entire, and He is our way and our truth and our life. The Church affirms the Eucharist to be "the source and summit" of our life, "For in the blessed Eucharist is contained the whole spiritual good of the Church, namely Christ himself, our

Pasch."[77]

More is needed for life than God's loving provision of our physical and material needs. We are human persons, made in the image of God and for God. Without God, and apart from Him, our lives remain hollow and adrift. Jesus left us with the very food that we absolutely and essentially need: God Himself, in intimate and personal communion with man. In Christ Himself we find our urgent need: "I am the bread of life; he who comes to me shall not hunger, and he who believes in me shall never thirst." (Jn 6:35)

We must have this bread! We must have Jesus! And we must remain with Him, very close to Him, even in Him, and He in us: "I am the vine, you are the branches. He who abides in me, and I in him, he it is that bears much fruit, for apart from me you can do nothing." (Jn 15:5) All the urgency now burning in the soul in this station, all the interior pressure to follow Him, come what may, and to bear fruit in His name, is reinforced with this sure realization. Apart from Him we can do nothing. Here, at the altar of the cross, with the commitment of interior consecration, we know that we must bear fruit. We stand here before His cross, but we will stand before His seat of judgment. It is only in the life of the Son that we can live our own vocation; it is only in Him that we come to know and to be who we are!

Mary in this station of Eucharist

In the hunger of this station, as we pray, "give us this day our daily bread," we gain new appreciation and love for Mary. Through her "yes" to the virginal conception of Jesus, through the formation of His sacred flesh in the pure sanctuary of her womb, Mary gave this saving bread to the world in the baby Jesus. Indeed, the flesh - the human nature - that He offered in perfect obedience to the Father for our sins - He received first from her immaculate, sinless womb. Through her care and love, with Joseph, she tended to this most holy bread as He grew toward His maturity and His sacrificial mission. At the cross she continued her nearness, her presence, her "yes" to the will of God, and so offered the most pure participation of a human person in the holy liturgy of her Son.

The *Catechism* explains that her role continues today in heaven, as she, "by her manifold intercession continues to bring us the gifts of eternal salvation."[78] Mary is most present to us in the Holy Mass: she, most wholly united with Him in the self-gift that is our daily bread. She continues to bring this saving bread to us, with all the spiritual gifts of eternal salvation that come to us in Christ.

In this station of the liturgy, then, we grow intimately close to Christ, receiving Him so intimately within our selves, our hearts, our bodies. He is the sustaining food and fire of life! He is the very substance of life. As we receive Him, so thankfully offering our own "yes" to His gift, we find there so close is Mary. In her quiet humility, she waits and serves, seeking only His honor and our salvation.

Examination of Conscience in the Fourth Station

As I pray, "Give us this day our daily bread," I ask myself: Do I want this bread for myself? Do I want this bread for us all? Do I want this bread daily? Do I want this bread today?

Do I want this bread for us all? This question challenges my style of living and my independence, my concern for the poor and my concern for the unity of the Church. First, I am called in Christ to a concern for the poor: the materially poor. I pray for the daily bread for the poor - is my life consistent with my prayer? Do I give to the poor? Do I excessively consume the resources of the world with immoderate desires and an extravagant lifestyle? Do I help the Church to be aware of the needs of the poor? Do I act in society, politics and government in ways that help the poor? Do I personally know any poor persons, being friend to them, showing them the respect and dignity that they deserve? Do I welcome eye contact, and smile at beggars on the street, acknowledging them as persons? Do I support Christian organizations of charity that work for and with the poor?

I am called to a concern for the spiritually poor. Do I work for the spiritual bread, for the spiritual hungers of my brothers and sisters around me? Am I a spokesman for the good news of Jesus Christ - an evangelist among my friends and neighbors and even family? Do I accept my part in the apostolate of the Church to bring good news to the poor? Do I exercise the gifts that God has given me, to pass on the Gospel to others?

I am called to see the one bread given for all, Jesus Christ. "Because there is one bread, we who are many are one body, for we all partake of the one bread." (1 Cor 10:17) Do I work in all ways that I can for the unity of all God's people in the one body? Do I know, in my heart, the indivisibility of the body of Christ, and always strive for the unity that Christ calls us into in Him? Do I ever treat or speak of non-Catholics disrespectfully, or arrogantly? Do I hold in my heart the desire of Jesus that we may all be one? "There is one body and one Spirit, just as you were called to the one hope that belongs to your call, one Lord, one faith, one baptism, one God and Father of us all, who is above all and through all and in all." (Eph 4: 4-6)

Do I fully open myself to the self-giving that consecration at the altar entails? Do I truly welcome, interiorly, the example of blessed and virgin Mary as heart-priest and humble servant? Hearing the condition for His own: "By this all men will know that you are my disciples, if you have love for one another," (Jn 13:35), am I indeed His disciple? Do men know that I follow Him, by my love for others? Do I do all that I can to enable that "one-another" love among all Christians, that His light might shine in this dark world?

<u>Prayer</u> [79]

Father, we thank and praise you for the gift of your Son, our bread from heaven. Give us the grace to receive Him fully, humbly, obediently.

We pray together this prayer of St. Thomas Aquinas, celebrating the gift of God in Holy Eucharist:

Godhead here in hiding, whom I do adore

Masked by these bare shadows,

shape and nothing more,

See, Lord, at thy service low

lies here a heart

Lost, all lost in wonder at the God thou art.

Seeing, touching, tasting

are in thee deceived;

How says trusty hearing?

that shall be believed;

What God's Son has told me,

take for truth I do;

Truth himself speaks truly

or there's nothing true.

St. Thomas Aquinas, pray for us. Amen.

Chapter 9. The Fifth Station: Thy will be done on earth as it is in heaven.

The Station of Consecration in Suffering

The fifth station of the interior liturgy is the station of anointing in suffering. The prayer here is, "Thy will be done on earth as it is in heaven." The sacramental grace here prayed for, and given, is the grace of the Anointing of the Sick. This station corresponds to that fifth mansion within the soul in the *Interior Castle*, seen by St. Teresa of Avila.[80] The prayer of contemplation received here is described as the prayer of union.

In the fifth mansions of the interior castle, Teresa wrote of a prayer-relationship of deep spiritual delights. These authentic delights come, she teaches, from a deep acceptance of God's will. His will is not mysterious: His will is love. The love shared in these fifth mansions of the soul, Teresa writes, is the love of the soul for her Lord, which has reached the stage of a joining of hands with the beloved. Here then we understand already a certain significance of the petition of this station of the liturgy, "Thy will be done on earth as it is in heaven." Hands join to share labors. Hands join in a common will and intent. Hands join in anticipation of the deeper and more complete union to come, in the deeper mansions of St. Teresa, and in the further stations of the interior liturgy now proceeding.

In this station of the interior liturgy, we continue to stand before the altar which is His cross, still in the great movement of the liturgy of consecration. We stand with the beloved disciple and Mary the mother of Jesus, looking upon the terrible sacrifice of the Son. We see Jesus, yet in the blessed gift of contemplative gaze, we look through the cross as if into and through an icon, a window to the heavens, and so into the holy will of God. Through that bloody self-offering, most pure gift of loving obedience, we ponder and behold glory. Through the crucified one on earth, we see into the transcendent glory of the eternal will of God in heaven. Here is the mystery of divine love, and our invitation to life.

> I appeal to you therefore, brethren, by the mercies of God, to present your bodies as a living sacrifice, holy and acceptable to God, which is your spiritual worship. Do not be conformed to this world but be transformed by the renewal of your mind, that you may prove what is the will of God, what is good and acceptable and perfect.[81]

The cross is so different in transparency! In the union of contemplation, which is His gift in this station, all creation is seen differently – and here, at the foot of the cross, we gaze into the Sacred Heart of Jesus crucified to behold the loving communion of Father and Son. The surface of the crucifixion pronounces "yes": thy will be done on earth! The interiority of this act, its deepest mystery and meaning, whispers the "yes": as it is in heaven.

The cross is so poorly understood from its exterior. In the beginning of our liturgy, we heard the words but dismissed them quickly: "If anyone wishes to come after me, let him deny himself and take up his cross daily and follow me." (Lk 9:23) As Peter and the others, we could not comprehend this; we could not see into the interiority of the cross to the glory therein. Outside, there is pain, distress, loss, death. Within, there is the burning bush that is not consumed, there is glory, there is eternal life.

Mary in this station of anointing

To stand at the foot of the cross is to stand alongside Mary, for she was there first. We are bound to her and with her in the mystical family, by the words of Christ: "Behold your mother." She is bound maternally to us and to all beloved disciples: "Behold your son." Mary had thirty years before this hour of agony to meditate upon the words prophesied to her by Simeon, "and a sword will pierce through your own heart also." (Lk 2:35) Through those thirty years, Jesus was pleased to submit to her and to Joseph as an obedient son. Mary was given a period of time to see the Christ grow and mature with her, ever approaching the mystery of His mission. She, in those thirty years before the sword would come most fully to pierce her, "kept all these things in her heart." (Lk 2:51)

There is a sign for us in this station of anointing, then, through Mary. As Jesus was obedient to her, awaiting the hour of His vocation, so also the first apostles were commanded to wait, "until you are clothed with power from on high." (Lk 24:49) The second great movement of Christ's liturgy is not the final one! The apostles were to wait for the divine empowering that would enflame the Church with the zeal of the Holy Spirit: this would come at Pentecost, when the liturgy of communion would begin. So also Jesus waited, until the appointed time, and was submitted to Mary.

In this time of consecration, then, there is the time of humble waiting. We wait, interiorly and in prayer with Mary, as did the apostles and the others in the upper room awaiting "the promise." (Acts 1:4, 14) If we would offer ourselves to the will of God on earth, as it is in heaven, we must wait for the empowering promise of the Father. We wait with the Church, and we wait with Mary, together in prayer.

The Anointing of the Sick –
the Sacrament of the Fifth Station

The sacrament that specifically illuminates this station, revealing its meaning, is the sacrament of Anointing of the Sick. As Christ was anointed in His suffering on the cross, so the soul at this station, gazing upon Him and in a mysterious way drawn into union with His sacrifice, is also anointed.

Here at the altar of the cross, the Christian encounters the suffering Christ - indeed, the dying Christ. This great contradiction to the thinking of the world is therefore a great trial and crisis for the faithful. Here, then, is also an opportunity for the evil one to challenge and to sow seeds of doubt and even despair. It is crucially important to the soul, in the interior liturgy here at the cross, to receive the grace of anointing to enable us to see through the suffering to the glory of the will of God in heaven.

> The first grace of this sacrament is one of strengthening, peace and courage to overcome the difficulties that go with the condition of serious illness or the frailty of old age. This grace is a gift of the Holy Spirit, who renews trust and faith in God and strengthens against the temptations of the evil one, the temptation to discouragement and anguish in the face of death.[82]

The evil one does tempt us to discouragement and anguish in the face of suffering and death! Here, at the cross of Christ, the evil one speaks through the criminal hanging there beside Him, "Are you not the Christ? Save yourself and us!" (Lk 23:39) It is through fear of death that the evil one binds us and paralyzes us in unholy dread, subjecting us to lifelong bondage. (Heb 2:15) Here again he accuses and tempts and tries to destroy. The grace of God renews strength and trust, despite the suffering.

The grace of God here, in this crucial station of the interior liturgy so near to the passion, also gives us a certain union with this mystery of the passion of Christ.

> By the grace of this sacrament the sick person receives the strength and the gift of uniting himself more closely to Christ's Passion: in a certain way he is consecrated to bear fruit by configuration to the Savior's redemptive Passion. Suffering, a consequence of original sin, acquires a new meaning; it becomes a participation in the saving work of Jesus.[83]

We see then how configured to this station is the grace of this sacrament! Peering through, as it were, the agony of Jesus on His cross, the saving grace of Christ begins to configure us to His suffering! When we are invited into the life of Christ, and invited mysteriously to carry our cross behind Him, we are also invited into this profoundly mysterious participation in His redemptive outpouring in love. Indeed, we begin to understand love, as we never have before, in its most intimate meaning in self-gift. Jesus did not "merely" suffer - He gave Himself for us, whatever the cost. This is our vocation, heard anew in this station of suffering but beyond suffering - our vocation is to love.

As we pray, "thy will be done on earth as it is in heaven," we peer through the obedience of Jesus on the cross to the holy will in heaven. We look past to the loving Father to Whom Jesus always submitted. Through the icon of His cross, we ponder further, to the divine mystery in the heavens: the eternal kenosis of the Son in love for the Father. Here is the station of consecration unto suffering, whatever the cost, for the sake of the kingdom.

The will of God in heaven is the defining truth that orients all creation, and that illuminates for us human persons the way of life. Jesus lived the life of truth as man, obedient in all matters to the Father - even as He has for all eternity always submitted Himself to the Father as only-begotten Son. It is there, in the infinite mystery of the Trinity - in the mystery of the inner life of God as He is in three Persons, yet one God, that the will of God "in heaven" is lived fully and completely. Toward this divine mystery we must gaze humbly and hungrily seeking our meaning in this petition.

It is through this petition that all human suffering becomes more intelligible. I must suffer, because you have sinned. You must suffer, because I have sinned. Every human person must suffer, because we are bound together by a truth that cannot be broken, the truth of human solidarity and union. We are made for communion in love! If we refuse this truth, if we refuse communion in love, we die in the barren and empty wasteland of lies. If we seek to save our lives, we lose them. Our vocation, as human persons, is love. If, in grace, we see through the suffering of His cross to the communion of love that the cross declares, and seeing, and hearing, we believe, then we live. If we can hear as if by name His most personal call to each of us, if in the dark knowing of faith we utter our own "yes", we live. In our own self-offering with Him, in the union of our own cross with His, we live.

"… as it is in heaven":
Prelude to the Darkness before Communion

A most deep interior darkness is needed to come upon our own souls, in order to make possible the deeper embrace of truth that God desires for us. Our past understanding and experience are inadequate, and must be set aside as such. As Jesus said, "I go to prepare a place for you. And when I go and prepare a place for you, I will come again and will take you to myself, that where I am you may be also." (Jn 14:2-3) When Jesus left His disciples, He left them in a profound sorrow and darkness of soul. Yet this hard experience was necessary for them, to enable the new work, the new liturgy that makes possible their being with Him where He is. To prepare this place for Him within us, He needs to work in what is for us darkness.

A great interior darkness and experience of emptiness is needed, to initiate the final movement of the interior liturgy, the Liturgy of Communion. In the formation of the disciples of Jesus, they entered such a darkness first in the crisis of the Passion and the cross: this corresponds to the dark night of the senses, of St. John of the Cross. They entered a second time of profound darkness in the loss of the resurrected Christ, and in the days dispossessed of Him following His ascension into heaven. We may have more difficulty imagining the deep void in the souls of the disciples following the ascension, than their loss following His death on the cross. Yet the ascension was a different darkness, seeming to be even more dark, more penetrating and more searing within their souls, than the turmoil of the cross.

The dark night of the spirit

This beautiful phrase, "as it is in heaven," directs the heart longing for His holy will into the mystery of the heavens, where His will radiates from within the inner life of the Holy Trinity. There is a price to be paid, so to speak, by the soul longing for this most intimate communion in His will - the price is the searing darkness of the night of the spirit.

Why this purgation? Why this interior preparation for the Lord? Fr. Garrigou-Lagrange describes the "defects of the advanced" as a deeply rooted self-love, which impedes the union that both God and we desire. This self-love shows itself in voluntary distraction in prayer, spiritual dullness, arrogance and condescension toward others, and so on.[84] We simply are deficient in the simplicity, humility, and purity required for close and intimate relationship with God. God deals with these defects in a darkness, an aridity, an aloneness, a sense of barrenness called the dark night of the spirit.[85]

It is helpful to hear this phrase, "as it is in heaven", as an invitation to God, a cry for Him, an epiclesis and plea coming from the deepest center of the human heart. This center is the center and home of the self, the "I", the person. In the most personal center of being, where "I myself" live and am, there is a thirst, an imperative for communion. There in the heart are two faces of one truth: there I must wholly and authentically be who I am, and simultaneously, there I must wholly and authentically embrace the Other in the communion of love. This is my nature; this is human nature. It is here, in the most interior center of our being, that God makes His place in the dark night of the spirit.

The spirit of man longs for the defining truth of the life of the Holy Trinity. There, in the central mystery of our faith, is also the central mystery of our own nature, for we are created in the image of God. In the infinite furnace of love and communion that is the Holy Trinity - the inferno of Self-offering, given and received wholly, eternally - we find the meaning of our own lives. Each of us is to be one, an integrity; each finds this integrity in the out-pouring of his being in the communion of love.

We are called to pour out our all, the completeness of who we are, gladly and eagerly, for the good of the other - for friend, for enemy, for stranger. In Christ, in truth, no human person is enemy or stranger to us: any man is brother and friend. We are made for this, to be happily for the other, because this is how it is "in heaven." God, in the Persons of Father, and Son, and Holy Spirit, is ever completely for the Other. We are to pray for likeness to this divine heart, with eager self-gift, because this is the intention of God in our creation: in His image and likeness He made man.

The petition for His will, "as it is in heaven," offers our own heart to the potter's wheel, to be conformed to His likeness from within, to become a heart of love after the heart of God. Whatever remains here as defect, as impediment, is offered to the fires of cleansing: whether we fear to empty the whole cup, or whether we fear that that which we outpour is not true - it is all offered to Him in the dark furnace of the dark night. We most deeply want His will, as it is in heaven, and so we endure in the trials of this darkness. His light is shining still, though we cannot see it. We cannot see or feel, but we believe, and we hope, and we endure with trust in His love.

In the darkness we are not disturbed by all that is taken away from us, because we know it is God who has done this. We feel no consolations, no reassurance - but we wait, trusting Him who is greater than any feeling or sense of assurance. He does not seem to respond, to be present, to be listening - no matter: He is God. All that God has done and is doing is good. We trust Him; we entrust all to Him. How will I live? I trust Him. How will I die? I trust Him. What will I do? I trust Him. Who will ever know? God knows the truth of my heart. Whether no one on earth ever knows or understands or appreciates - whether I myself am finally right or wrong or deluded or faithful - finally, God is God and I entrust myself to Him.

Examination of Conscience in the Fifth Station

I pray, "thy will be done on earth as it is in heaven," and the holiness of the obedience of heaven humbles me. How partial, how incomplete is my own obedience? The story of the poor widow, who "put in all the living that she had," (Lk 21:4) confronts me and asks what I withhold from God. Do I seek to do less than all; do I try to find the least that I can do for God? Do I seek the fullness of His will, or rather, merely to not offend Him?

How different are these two ways! One way, the way of the saints, is to seek with all my heart to do what is most pleasing to God. Another way, a way of compromise, seeks to save my own life and pleasure in this world, while avoiding what might offend God. As I pray before the holy crucifix, I seek to see in the clear light of His witness, the will of God on earth for me, as it is in heaven. Show me here and now, Lord Jesus, how I might walk in love, and how I have failed to do so.

Prayer

Lord, make me an instrument of Thy peace;
where there is hatred, let me sow love;
where there is injury, pardon;
where there is doubt, faith;
where there is despair, hope;
where there is darkness, light;
and where there is sadness, joy.
O Divine Master,
grant that I may not so much seek
to be consoled as to console;
to be understood, as to understand;
to be loved, as to love;
for it is in giving that we receive,
it is in pardoning that we are pardoned,
and it is in dying that
we are born to eternal life.

St. Francis of Assisi, pray for us. Amen.

SECTION 3. THE THIRD MOVEMENT: THE LITURGY OF COMMUNION

The work of God, in the silent and empty desert of the dark night, has prepared us for this final liturgy in the soul: the liturgy of communion. All that there is for us as Christians awaits us, in a sense, in the liturgy of communion. Our discipleship in Christ has been ordered from the beginning to this time, to this movement of His saving work. This work in the interior liturgy corresponds, in traditional Catholic spirituality, to the stage of the perfect, or the unitive stage of the spiritual life.

This liturgy of communion corresponds with the work of the same name in the communal liturgy of Holy Mass, when we receive the sacred, real, substantially present Christ into ourselves: His body, blood, soul and divinity, the complete Christ. This movement of the interior liturgy corresponds also to that movement of God that He worked in the early Church at Pentecost, in the gift of the Holy Spirit, when they as human persons were "filled" with God the Holy Spirit. In the interior liturgy, in this third movement, the presence of God in the soul of a human person is now different - here is the maturity of God's saving work, the time for fruitfulness. This is the movement of what is called "perfection" - not a perfection static or dead but living, fruitful, human and loving. This is the movement of the perfection of charity in the soul.

Mary in the Liturgy of Communion

The community of saints awaits us in this movement, with Mary their mother and ours. To understand the place of Mary for us in this liturgy, we must consider and understand virginity in the kingdom, and we must come to know better her Spouse the Holy Spirit. Mary is linked, in the divine plan, to the Holy Spirit. In her virginal openness to Him, the work of God could proceed. In her virginal "yes" to God, through the Holy Spirit, the saving incarnation of the Son could begin.

The Virgin Mary

We often hear virginity negatively, its meaning understood in terms of the absence of something. Adult voluntary virginity is, for most of us in this very sexually oriented culture, the strange denial of a fundamental human good. Virginity in its religious meaning in the communion of Christian faith, however, is a great good and a positive affirmation. Christian virginity within the virtue of charity is a most fertile communion with God in Christ.

The *Catechism* describes the virginity of Mary: " her virginity is the sign of her faith 'unadulterated by any doubt', and of her undivided gift of herself to God's will."[86] We can hear in this the two dimensions of virginity, the giving and the receiving. Mary's faith, her openness to God, to receive and accept His will for her, was complete. No doubt, no reservation stood between her and God. On her side, she was open to receive whatever God in His trusted love would send her or ask of her. This is the "receiving" dimension of her virginity.

Mary was also completely given to God in trust and in love. Her gift of self was undivided; her response to God was ready: an ever-present "yes". Mary shows us, with a constancy enabled by the abundant grace of God, the beauty of one truly available to Him. This is the "giving" dimension of her virginity: Mary gave of herself, all of herself, completely, to God and His will.

This positive aspect of virginity must be understood, if we are to understand Mary. The virginity of Mary is not merely the absence of sexual love with a man, it is the presence of complete love for God - and complete willingness to follow this love for God wherever it led. Her openness to God, the giving and receiving that defines communion, is pure and free in her. Because our words and our hearts are tainted by concupiscence, we easily fall short in understanding the simplicity of Mary, as we fail to understand the true meaning of Christian virginity in love.

Virginity in love is portrayed to us most perfectly in Mary. God, through Mary, explains virginity to us in her life-example, appropriately in the context of the divine incarnation. Mary showed us, for the first time, the human meaning of kenosis. She showed us what it means to fully offer oneself in the obedience of faith and love. Because of this - because of Mary - a great veil was drawn back for men, although this veil could never have been penetrated before the self-offering of Christ on His cross. The sacrifice of Christ defines for us kenosis; Mary shows us the most perfect human example. The grace of His Self-gift, applied as it was to Mary in anticipation of His Passion, enabled Mary to live the truth of this love, fully humanly, and so to show us all our own vocations.

Mary and the Holy Spirit

In God the Holy Trinity, we hear of the infinite dynamo of kenosis, of Self-gift, of Self-outpoured to the Other in love. God is an infinite fireball of love, symbolized so humbly in the burning bush revealed to Moses. God is an expanse beyond measure of divine Gift offered and received. The Father in eternal Self outpoured, eternally begets His Son. The Son, in eternal submission and obedience, forever doing what is pleasing to the Father (Jn 8:29), in the timeless *now*, outpours Himself: God, as Son. The Holy Spirit, eternally proceeding from the Father and the Son, is forever Love, and Gift, in the communion that is God.

Man "is the only creature on earth which God willed for

itself," and yet he "cannot fully find himself except through a sincere gift of himself."[87] In the image of this divine paradox we are made: we, too, exist in dignity because we are; we, too, are ourselves only in kenosis, in self-gift. Mary, in her persistent and humble "yes" to God, reveals to us the great mystery of the divine nature, in her excellently human way.

We are invited to follow the fullness of giving and receiving, characterizing the virginity of Mary, to its divine origin in God. To understand human Christian virginity, we must peer through Mary our icon, into the Holy Trinity. There, in the eternal Self-giving and mutual embrace within God in His inner life, we come to understand finally the potent fecundity of virginity in Christ. Mary is most beautifully an icon for us: supremely both virgin and fruitful mother. Mary, like an icon, becomes transparent for us and reveals for us the eternal generation of Persons within the Holy Trinity. The perpetual virginity of Mary points us to God, and her ever-faithful maternity reveals the will of God, that we should go forth and bear fruit, and that the fruit of us should abide.

Can we not see how this faithful virginity of Mary, so beautifully imaging, humanly, the fruitful kenosis of God the Holy Trinity, unknowingly invites the Holy Spirit to herself? How must He rejoice to find the divine image so faithfully lived! He whose name is Love, and Gift, finds in her the most perfect self-offering in love, possible for a human person. The *Catechism* states, "In the faith of his humble handmaid, the Gift of God found the acceptance he had awaited from the beginning of time."[88] The Holy Spirit is, in the inner life of God, eternally Gift[89] of the Father to the Son, in the communion of the Father with the Son. The Spirit finds in Mary the most pure human gift and giver, the most beautiful of all made in the divine image.

Prayer and Work in the Liturgy of Communion

Our prayer, in the liturgy of communion, is intensely Marian and at the same time intensely Trinitarian. There is a unity of these two theological terms, in one theological reality. The truth of our faith, in which we rest and act, is merely and entirely love. Communion in Christ is communion with Mary; communion in Christ is communion in God the Holy Trinity. Our prayer here, in this third movement of the interior liturgy, is a communion in her "yes", and our prayer as lived reflects her embrace of His will: through the power of the Holy Spirit, the life of Christ is brought into the world of men.

Prayer, in the liturgy of communion, is the perfection of charity; it is the embrace of the will of God in the work of the kingdom; it is the marital union of the soul with the divine Spouse. Prayer and work in this movement shows the two components so well-represented in the history of our saints, the two facets of charity, the contemplative and the active.

Charity - our participation in the mystery of Trinitarian love - finds beautiful human expression in this third movement of the interior liturgy. Charity is experienced interiorly, in the mutual embrace of the soul with God in contemplative prayer, and charity is expressed exteriorly, in those acts of love that are the mission of the Church. Our personal vocation is simple: to love. Our mission as Church is simple: to love. Our prayer is meant to be, and finally is, union with Him. Prayer is nothing other than this: union with God.[90] Our apostolate, our work for Him, is nothing other than our acts of love for men and women in His holy name. Here, in the final saving movement of God at work in the soul, here in the third great movement of His liturgy, are these two expressions - the active and the contemplative - condensed in the two stations: "thy kingdom come", and "hallowed be thy name."

Chapter 10. The Sixth Station: Thy kingdom come.

The Station of Ecclesial Communion

The sixth station of the interior liturgy is the station of new love for, and communion with, holy Church. The prayer here is, "Thy kingdom come." The grace here prayed for, and given, is a grace corresponding in a sense to the sacrament of Holy Orders. This station corresponds to that sixth mansion within the soul in the *Interior Castle*, seen by St. Teresa of Avila.[91] The prayer of contemplation received here is described as the prayer of transforming union.

In the sixth mansions of the interior castle, St. Teresa describes an experience of profound suffering, yet with joy, in Christ. In these mansions, the soul becomes betrothed to Christ the Beloved. The persons in these mansions become forgetful of self, contemptuous of any existence outside of Christ, and profoundly devoted to the life in union with Him. Here, the person has entered the sixth station of the interior liturgy. Here, the prayer of the soul is that petition of the *Our Father*, "Thy kingdom come."

The prayer, "thy kingdom come," is an opening of the soul to the full rule of God, both personally – to rule in my own life – and beyond the personal – to rule as king throughout His entire universe. The prayer is also a petition to hasten that rule: let it come now! "Thy kingdom come," welcomes the coming of that kingdom that has been "at hand" now for two millennia. The kingdom has been personally near – "at hand" – before now, even from the very beginning of the work of Christ in the soul. Here, in the third movement of the liturgy, His nearness is of a different kind: more interior, more immediate, more intimate.

It is part of a great mystery that a person can have Christ

truly within him, by virtue of the grace of Baptism and the other sacraments - from the very start of the liturgy - and yet not experience this. We receive Him by faith in the beginning of the interior liturgy, in those sacraments of initiation; we experience Him in a wholly new way in the second movement of the liturgy, at the altar within. Here, as He begins the third movement of His work, He confirms His interior presence with an abiding constancy. This constancy, this persisting communion, brings a new force within us to the imperatives of His life: His imperatives are now ours. It is not that His will should be done: it must be done, it shall be done.

The kingdom that, before, was in the distant future for us - a point out in eternity - has now become very, very near. He Himself is very near: He is here, He is now, His kingdom is at the very door. This realization and knowledge brings several implications. One is the now magnified importance of the Church: His Church is His kingdom now begun on earth. This interior station greatly amplifies love in us for His Church: a fervent, authentic, zealous love. Love for the Church has been growing through the whole liturgy, beginning first in a love mostly of need and dependency, but later growing toward a deep familial love, and true embrace of community. Here, in the third movement of the interior liturgy, love for the Church grows to its fullness. Love for His Church is enflamed in this new and immediate and persistent presence within us: He is here, and His Sacred Heart burns with His love for His Bride. The Church is wholly and personally His. She is His Body on this earth; she is His Bride in the kingdom yet to come. The Church is His holy Spouse, His most Beloved who is now being prepared for the great wedding feast of the Lamb.

Mary and Peter together

In this fullness of love now aroused for the Church, we see a certain merging of the Marian and the Petrine dimensions of the Church. The maternal loving care of Mary and the apostolic loving shepherding of Peter come together on behalf of the people of God. The apostolic love of Peter was aroused in him by the risen Christ, as he was told, "Feed my lambs," "Tend my sheep", "Feed my sheep." (Jn 21: 15, 16, 17) The maternal love of Mary was opened in fullness toward the whole Church when she was told in the agony of the cross, "Behold your son."

This focussed and intentional love for the Church is the first mark of the ecclesial spirit freshly stirred to action in this station of the interior liturgy. This nurturing care has its interior and exterior dimensions, perhaps somewhat described as the Marian and the Petrine dimensions, yet they are intimately one. Especially here in the sixth station of the interior liturgy, these interior and exterior facets are no more than dimensions of one calling, not at all two different vocations.

There are some who are called most strongly into the contemplative life - to open their own hearts most personally to the blazing furnace of the Sacred Heart, in the name of His Bride, the holy Church. These have a hidden role, in a hidden life, to listen at His breast and to whisper in His ear for us all. These, in imitation of Mary, serve in an interior priesthood of prayer, of intercession, of waiting.

Others are called most strongly to the works of the Church, to provide her feet and hands, her voice and labors, her witness and presence among men in the world. These, in a more exterior or "apostolic" role, must be seen and not hidden, so that their light might shine before men, that they might give glory to the Father in heaven. (Mt 5:16)

In truth all are called, in imitation of Jesus, to both the interior dimension of His life and to its outward expression - to prayer before the Father and to ministry before men. Even the most secluded contemplative hermit is bearing witness to others, in quiet and mystical ways. Even the most outward worker in ministry treasures his interior communion with Christ.

First, the re-evangelization

There is a difference between the reprovals or corrections given to a child because of love for the child, and those given through a self-love in the adult. It costs little, and it profits little, to correct flaws and failures in the Church from a self-righteous position of judgment. Such condescending, self-righteous disapproval of others in the Church is a temptation in previous stations of the interior liturgy, especially in the very beginning, and then again in the beginning of the second movement. In the first and second stations, and perhaps more strongly in the fourth station, there may be temptations to see clearly (we think) the splinters in our brother's eye (Mt 7:3), and yet to be unconscious of the logs in our own eyes. In this station, a much different sense is awakened through grace in the soul, the grace of authentic maternal and paternal love for the Church on behalf of Christ.

There are needs in the Church, crying out for attention! The Church in our time is confused by many forces outside of us as well as among us, forces that are not of Christ. Many of us are ignorant of some of the most fundamental foundations of the Faith: the Person and nature of Jesus Christ, the meaning of Eucharist, the gift of the Magisterium, the priesthood of the laity, the sanctity of the home, the treasure of children, the meaning of sexuality, the dignity of the human person - the list could go on for pages. There is a widespread ignorance of the Faith among the members, and no easy way is in sight to correct it! We are all too busy, too preoccupied with the secular demands upon us, to give essential attention to the more important spiritual realities.

Time must be made for God! The members must be led to see that a famine has come upon us - not because there is no bread, but because we don't know where to find it and we don't know how to receive it. We don't even know what is bread for us any more, we have become so filled and so numbed by the things of the world. Inwardly we languish in deep, deep hunger; outwardly we run about here and there, trying to fill ourselves with what is not bread.

What will it take, to awaken the people? This is the question that haunts the soul in this station of the interior liturgy, praying "thy kingdom come." How, oh Lord, am I to give myself to this petition? How am I to speak to your Church, that she might hear and arise?

<u>The call into one</u>

Love for the Church requires the work of reunion, of regathering those now scattered because of sin. It is sin that keeps us apart from one another, just as it is sin that keeps us apart from God. Our enemy in the work of ecumenism, then, is sin. Why is ecumenism so important a concern, for all who would serve and love the Church? Because it is so important to Christ and to His Gospel.

Jesus has placed before us the inseparable link connecting the unity in love among Christians, and the effectiveness of our apostolate in the world. He said, "A new commandment I give to you, that you love one another; even as I have loved you, that you also love one another. By this all men will know that you are my disciples, if you have love for one another." (John 13:34-35) Our mutual love in Christ is the sign of our authenticity as Christians. If we do not bear witness to Christ with the evidence of unity in love, then our words are, as Paul said, "as a noisy gong or a clanging cymbal." (1 Cor 13:1)

The Church has a mission in this world: to share in the

liturgy, the life, the love, the suffering of Christ. With one voice we are to preach one truth; in one intention we are to go out to the entire world in the saving name of Jesus. Will they recognize the truth of God in our message? Will they recognize the love of God in our ministry? Will they hear and see Jesus in us? Jesus prayed that it might be so: "I do not pray for these only, but also for those who believe in me through their word, that they may all be one; even as thou, Father, art in me, and I in thee, that they also may be in us, so that the world may believe that thou hast sent me." (Jn 17: 20-21)

The holiness and unity of the Church is personally the burden of the heart of one in this station of the interior liturgy. Praying, "thy kingdom come," the heart-priest looks upon the Bride of Christ, the Church. Indeed, he takes upon his own heart this same love, "as Christ loved the church and gave himself up for her, that he might sanctify her, having cleansed her by the washing of water with the word, that he might present the church to himself in splendor, without spot or wrinkle or any such thing, that she might be holy and without blemish." (Eph 5: 25-27)

The Great Mission

Jesus came not merely to gather some people out from the world. He did gather but few: twelve, and one was to be lost. But this small community, with a few women and others, would be the seed of a radical, new and divine movement among men: ambassadors of the Messiah, the Body of Christ. Through this Church the life of Christ would be made available to men. These Jesus sent in His name, commanding them:

> Go therefore and make disciples of all nations, baptizing them in the name of the Father and of the Son and of the Holy Spirit, teaching them to observe all that I have commanded you; and lo, I am with you always, to the close of the age.[92]

The world is confused in darkness and error, they need the

light and truth of Christ: make disciples among them! They languish in the coldness of indifference and even hatred: show them love! Wash them in the great mystery of divine love: Father, Son and Holy Spirit! They stumble in contradictions and conflict even within themselves: gather them into faithful integrity! Teach them to observe all that I have commanded you, the completeness of My gift. This will require your whole life, and generations of whole lives. Work patiently, confidently, courageously: I am with you always, to the close of the age.

The great saving work of Jesus Christ has been to bring the reign of God to humanity - first from within, within the sacred humanity of His own flesh, and then through that flesh to others. Jesus has opened the kingdom of God to man through His own self-gift, through His own most holy liturgy. In this prayer, we welcome and invite that kingdom, that work, into ourselves and upon the whole world.

In the interior liturgy, within my soul and yours, this prayer, "thy kingdom come," implies our own cooperation and collaboration in His work. This petition, in this sixth station, offers and contributes our flesh also with His, in the continuing communal liturgy of the Church. Here we include our own "yes", and our bodies also, in the proclamation of the gospel: "the kingdom of God is at hand." (Mt 4:17) We call down His kingdom, in its fullness, and may it be now! We also offer ourselves, and immediately: "Here am I! Send me." (Is 6:8) That is, in calling forth His kingdom, here and now, we also present ourselves, today, as laborers for it and in it.

> And his gifts were ... to equip the saints for the work of ministry, for building up the body of Christ, until we all attain to the unity of the faith and of the knowledge of the Son of God, to mature manhood, to the measure of the stature of the fullness of Christ....[93]

The Church

In this petition, "thy kingdom come," we offer ourselves to the liturgy of Christ, to the work of bringing among us His kingdom. One could say, then, that here we offer ourselves to Jesus particularly and explicitly through His Church, which is the kingdom already begun on earth. This prayer invites us into the interiority of the Church, the Bride of Christ, where the light of the kingdom already shines. This prayer forms in us a proper love for the Church. To pray "thy kingdom come," indeed requires of us a fervent and pure love for the Church. The kingdom is anticipated in His Church, and is begun already in her and through her. It is only through the personal, pure and genuine love for this beloved bride of our Lord, that these words can be uttered in integrity. It is through authentic love for the Church that our humble works are good works, building her up and not tearing her down.

There are some with only an exterior sense of the Church, seeing only her structure, her human element. They do not see within, to the communion among her members, to her union with Christ her Spouse. They are blind to the mystery that is crucial to her meaning and essence. They fail to perceive that beauty radiating from her heart one with the heart of Christ, becoming in Him a blazing furnace of divine love for the people of God. They do not see this love; they do not see her life.

Our prayer for the kingdom must pass through the Church. The kingdom is entrusted to the Church, and awaits her part in the divine work. Our prayer for the kingdom, here in this sixth station of our interior liturgy, is most intimately bound to the holy work, the liturgy, of the Church.

The nearness of Mary

As we pray, "thy kingdom come," we look attentively to the Church. As we grow in prayer, our attentive look becomes a longing gaze, a waiting upon God, our "yes" in contemplative communion with the Lord. It is His Church, His body, and in the heart-center of this body is Mary: my mother, your mother, mother of the whole Christ.

In the liturgy of communion, Marian devotion and trinitarian devotion are enflamed together in the heart, and illuminated in their union in the simple clear light of Christ. In this liturgy of the kingdom, we see Mary and know that Mary is the Church. In the coming liturgy of the name, we see Mary now forever in trinitarian covenant: mother of Christ the Son, spouse of the Holy Spirit, most holy and immaculate daughter of the Father.

Mary is the Church. The *Catechism*, recalling Vatican II, teaches that Mary is the image of our call:

> In her we contemplate what the Church already is in her mystery on her own "pilgrimage of faith," and what she will be in the homeland at the end of her journey. There, "in the glory of the Most Holy and Undivided Trinity," "in the communion of all the saints,"[LG 69] the Church is awaited by the one she venerates as Mother of her Lord and as her own mother.

> In the meantime the Mother of Jesus, in the glory which she possesses in body and soul in heaven, is the image and beginning of the Church as it is to be perfected in the world to come. Likewise she shines forth on earth until the day of the Lord shall come, a sign of certain hope and comfort to the pilgrim People of God. [LG 68; Cf. 2 Pet 3:10] [94]

To seek Jesus through Mary, to consecrate ourselves to Jesus through Mary as St. Louis de Montfort invites us to do, is to seek Him through His consecrated Body the Church, for Mary is ever the immaculate human heart of His Church. If we would see the Church, His mystical Body, we would see Mary, her image and beginning and perfection, as the *Catechism* teaches. If we would submit ourselves to the Church, as Christ wills, then we would submit ourselves to Mary as He did in the years before His hour. If we would submit ourselves to Christ, we would offer ourselves in union with Mary and with the whole Church as He did on the cross, and as He does in every Mass.

Holy Orders - the Sacrament of the Sixth Station

The sacrament that specifically illuminates this station, revealing its inner meaning, is the sacrament of Orders. This sixth station is of consecration unto the service of the kingdom; the sacrament of Orders pronounces, in the ministries of those who receive its grace, this same calling: "thy kingdom come!"

The sacrament of Orders consecrates specifically deacons, priests and bishops to the ministerial work at the service of the common priesthood in which all the faithful participate. The common priesthood of us all "is exercised by the unfolding of baptismal grace - a life of faith, hope and charity, a life according to the spirit."[95] The ministerial priesthood is the means by which Christ builds up his people, His Church, His kingdom for that common priesthood.

We are all called into the ministry of Christ as priest, as prophet, as king by virtue of our Baptism. In the unfolding work of Christ in the soul, this vocation grows and develops, revealing gradually and more clearly as the liturgy progresses, our part in His saving work. In this station of the interior liturgy, Christ awakens in the Christian a glimpse, if not a vision, of the glory of His kingdom and the beauty of His Bride. What love for His Church is stirred in the heart, in this station! How beautiful she is! Even in her imperfections, and her sins, and her divisions, and her contradictions - there, within, the glory of the intention of God shines. The virgin and immaculate Mary, humble and magnificent, radiates within the Church as beginning and as end.

This is the station of founders and foundresses of orders,

of movements, of institutes. This is the station of renewal, and leaders of renewal. This is the station of saints and martyrs who would live or die for the good of the kingdom, for the honor of the blessed spouse of Christ. This is the station of those who would serve the Church as humble servants, because of love.

Witnesses and workers

The ministry of the heart-priest in this sixth station of the interior liturgy is characterized within by tears and joy, and without by blood and labors. How we need such servants of love! How we need the anointed shepherding of Peter, and the maternal graces of Mary. The Church needs authentic human ministry, empowered by the Spirit of God: this is the ministry of the heart-priest, serving in communion with his Lord.

The perfect joy of St. Francis

There is a beautiful story from the life of St. Francis of Assisi that illustrates the heart and mind of a soul who is living in the third great movement of the interior liturgy. It is perhaps not possible to declare whether Francis was in his sixth station or seventh station of his own interior liturgy, when this occurred. It is possible to say that this discourse came from a person in the liturgy of communion, in at least the sixth station of the interior liturgy.

Francis called Brother Leo to him, and announced that he would teach him what perfect joy is. Faithful and obedient Brother Leo, of course, was eager to hear and to learn. Francis first describes a great surge in membership in their new order, the Order of Friars Minor. Francis listed the respected and the honored as those flocking to join the Order: "all the doctors of Paris ... all the bishops, archbishops, and prelates of the whole world, ... the kings of France and England," yet then concluded that this would not be perfect joy.

He continued, supposing that all the faithless had been converted by the work of the friars, that the friars had received powerful charismatic gifts, such as the gift of miracles, and to heal, and to give sight to the blind, and speech to the dumb. Francis continued, supposing his order to be able to give hearing to the deaf, mobility to the crippled, life to men dead for days, with the power to know the future, and the secret consciences of men. His list and description continued to suppose that they had knowledge of everything ever written in the history of man, and they could know the paths of the stars, the places of all buried treasure, the natures of all creatures animate and inanimate! He said again to Brother Leo, that this would still not be perfect joy.

We can understand the frustration of Brother Leo! He exclaimed, "Father! For the love of God, please tell me then just what is perfect joy?"

Francis then began to describe a situation that only a most mature Christian could receive well. He said that Brother Leo should imagine that Francis had just returned from a trip, in the darkness of a cold winter night. He has icicles hanging from his habit, cutting his legs such that they are bleeding. Francis is dirty, covered with this ice and snow, hungry and cold. He arrives at the friary and knocks at the door, calling for someone to open for a long time. When the porter finally finds the time to come to the door, he does not believe that it is really Francis calling to come in. He yells at poor Francis through the door, insulting him, threatening him, and warning him to go away.

Francis then begs him and implores him to open and let him in from the cold harsh night. Just then, he does open - but to attack Francis, still not recognizing him, beating him with a wooden club and hurting him, dragging him away through the snow. Here, Francis finally concludes his lesson to Brother Leo: "Well, Leo, if I am able to bear all this for love of God, not only with patience but with happiness, convinced that I deserve no other treatment, know, remember, and write down on your paper, God's Little Sheep, that at last I have found perfect joy."[96]

Here is a Christian in joyful imitation of Christ, even unto the suffering of the cross. A heart-priest knows that love is not always teaching with words, nor does it seek the consolations of gratitude. Love means being for the other, whatever the cost.

When Martha, distracted with much serving, was pointed by Jesus toward her sister Mary who listened at His feet, she was being directed to the essential foundation needed for her true service to Christ. (Lk 10:38-42) Ministry must be the fruit of true communion in Christ, which begins in prayer. Here, in the station of priestly service, the fruit of communion in Christ manifests His life in beautiful human ministries. Interiorly and exteriorly, the life of Christ burns and radiates His light. In prayer and in work, it is Christ abiding and acting. "I have been crucified with Christ; it is no longer I who live, but Christ who lives in me; and the life I now live in the flesh I live by faith in the Son of God, who loved me and gave himself for me." (Gal 2:20)

Examination of Conscience in the Sixth Station

Is my life a life of communion in Christ? Is my consecration in His Body, His Church, a living, active and fruitful one? Is my self-gift one of integrity, completeness and simple trust? Do I, in truth, love the Church?

"Behold, I am the handmaid of the Lord; let it be to me according to your word." (Lk 1:38) God gave to Moses a glimpse into the divine name, "I AM." Absolute Being is inseparable from Absolute Love. Am I true to my most true being, in my loving? Mary's "I am" is immediately service, obedience, "yes" to God. Am I so transparent to His will and call? Do I withhold any of my self from Him? Am I truly open to His word to me? Is Christ the fruit of my faith? Do I treasure this faith within me, as well as give birth to this faith, in good works in the world? Are there ways in which I refuse God my heart, my body, my time, my life?

"Finally, all of you, have unity of spirit, sympathy, love of the brethren, a tender heart and a humble mind." (1 Pet 3:8) Do I guard and protect the precious truth of unity of spirit? Do I in any way violate the unity of the faith, the unity in love in the Church? Do I in any way close my heart to my brothers and sisters, and so break the oneness of love? Do I in any way break unity with the hierarchy and magisterium of the Church through arrogance of mind and independence of heart? Do I seek to always form my conscience in unity with the Church, and live my conscience courageously? Do I live in faithful and active communion with the whole Christ, Head and Body, always carrying the cross behind Him?

Prayer:

Father, tear the veils from my eyes, that I may see Holy Church as you see her! Show me her wounds, where I may carry to her your healing love; show me her hungers, that I may beg you for her food. Show me her beauty in your eyes, that I may love her as you do; show me her glory, that I may serve her, and you in her, and that I may rejoice when I hear the voice of the Bridegroom come for her. Mary our mother, pray for us. Amen.

Chapter 11. The Seventh Station: Hallowed be thy name.

The Station of Personal Communion

The seventh station of the interior liturgy is the station of new union in Christ, corresponding to holy marriage. The prayer here is "Hallowed be thy name." The grace here prayed for, and given, is the grace corresponding to the sacrament of Matrimony. This station corresponds to that seventh mansion within the soul in the *Interior Castle*, seen by St. Teresa of Avila.[97] The prayer of contemplation received here is described as the prayer of conforming union.

In this last and seventh mansions of the interior castle, St. Teresa sees the soul brought into spiritual marriage with the Lord, the Beloved. Here is found the most intimate of unions with God in Christ, as the Holy Trinity - Father, Son and Holy Spirit - is known to dwell within the soul. It is here, in the seventh and ultimate station of the interior liturgy, that the culmination of His saving work in persons on earth finds expression. This most complete of unions with Christ, possible this side of glory in heaven, is union in His name. The prayer of this station is the petition of the *Our Father*, "Hallowed be thy name."

The interior liturgy began in the name, and concludes in the name. In the beginning in Baptism, the sacrament of the first station, we were baptized in the name of the Father, and of the Son, and of the Holy Spirit. Here in the final station of the interior liturgy, His work concludes as we pray, "hallowed be thy name." The entire liturgy of Christ is the work He has done in the name: "While I was with them, I kept them in thy name, which thou hast given me...." (Jn 17:12) His work is to gather us and guard us in this saving and holy name: "I made known to them thy name, and I will make it known, that the love with which thou hast loved me may be in them, and I in them." (Jn 17:26)

The Mystery of the Name

If we can even begin to see the holiness and glory of this name! This name is the radiance of His splendor, the center of all the holy mysteries of God. This name is life! If we are to have life, it will be in this name: "these are written that you may believe that Jesus is the Christ, the Son of God, and that believing you may have life in his name." (Jn 20:31)

The holy name of God is not "God". The name of the Father is more than "Father"; the name of the Son is more than "Son"; the name of the Spirit is more than "Spirit." There is one name. There are three Persons, whose intimate communion in love is suggested in the names of their relations among themselves – but the relationships can only suggest to us the infinite depth of their communion in love. The Father is "Father" because He is Father of the Son. The Son is "Son" because He is Son of the Father. Yet even these two relations are incomplete to name God, although they are, each, fully God. The communion of Father with Son is also Person: He is "Holy Spirit", He is Love, He is Gift.

The infinite mystery of God in Himself, in His inner life and being, requires three Persons in relation to communicate – and yet there is one God; there is one name. We are baptized into the one name – the name possessed by the Father, for it is His name, and of the Son, for it is His name given Him by the Father, and of the Holy Spirit, for it is His name also, from the Father and the Son.

The one name, the name of God cloaked in infinite mystery, is the name to be hallowed. This name is our life and our fecundity, our joy: "Hitherto you have asked nothing in my name; ask, and you will receive, that your joy may be full." (Jn 16:24) In this name we are sent: our mission, our apostolate, our purpose in this world is contained in the name: "Go therefore and make disciples of all nations, baptizing them in the name of the Father and of the Son and of the Holy Spirit...." (Mt 28:19)

This name, which is the eternal communion of Persons, the Holy Trinity, is the crucial center of truth and life, of being and becoming:

> The mystery of the Most Holy Trinity is the central mystery of Christian faith and life. It is the mystery of God in himself. It is therefore the source of all the other mysteries of faith, the light that enlightens them. It is the most fundamental and essential teaching in the "hierarchy of the truths of faith". The whole history of salvation is identical with the history of the way and the means by which the one true God, Father, Son and Holy Spirit, reveals himself to men "and reconciles and unites with himself those who turn away from sin".[98]

The power and significance of this petition is hidden in its simplicity - how like our God, who gave the prayer to us! This petition is first and last among the seven petitions of the *Our Father* - first in prayer and primacy of desire, last in station and fulfillment. This petition is unique, within the prayer that has stature which cannot be surpassed.

First we must hear the rightful regard of the Church for this prayer, the *Our Father*. Quoting Tertullian, the *Catechism* asserts that, "The Lord's Prayer 'is truly the summary of the whole gospel.'" (2761) Augustine is cited in recognizing the unique completeness of the prayer: "Run through all the words of the holy prayers [in Scripture], and I do not think that you will find anything in them that is not contained and included in the Lord's Prayer." (2762) The *Catechism* sees that this remarkable prayer "is at the center of the Scriptures." (2774)

Scripture fulfilled in Christ: this is our "Good News." This Gospel is summarized in His Sermon on the Mount (Mt 5-7), and the *Our Father* "is at the center of this proclamation." (2763). Quoting St. Thomas Aquinas, we read that it is "the most perfect of prayers." (2763) It is "the quintessential prayer of the Church" (2776), "the fundamental Christian prayer." (2773)

From within the context of this high but due praise for the prayer itself, we read further that this particular petition, "Hallowed be thy name," the first petition of the seven, contains a unique gathering of all the petitions of the *Our Father*: "This petition embodies all the others."[99] The simple petition for the holiness of the holy name might conceal by its simplicity, the immense depth and meaning that it conveys.

In this modest and straightforward petition, two great mysteries are contained: first there is the mystery of the name of God, the meaning of His holy name in itself and for us. Second, there is the mystery of our gathering into His holiness – that is, the mystery of our salvation itself. The name of God is that deepest mystery of His Being: His name declares His innermost nature, out of which radiates His divine glory. We find in the *Catechism*,

> The holiness of God is the inaccessible center of his eternal mystery. What is revealed of it in creation and history, Scripture calls "glory," the radiance of his majesty.[100]

Again, the *Catechism* calls us to the two-fold importance of the petition, "Hallowed be thy name": "Beginning with this first petition to our Father, we are immersed in the innermost mystery of his Godhead and the drama of the salvation of our humanity." (2807) For our purposes in witnessing to the beauty of His interior liturgy, we see immediately the corresponding import to this saving work of God in the soul. In this station of the interior liturgy, the last of the seven stations of His redemptive work before our final gathering into Him in glory, we are brought face to face with the infinite mystery of His Being, His inner life, His nature. Additionally, illuminated so to speak by this glory, we are also immediately faced with the great mystery of our salvation itself: our vocation into that holiness, that life, that divine presence in glory. Here we recognize our call into His holy life - His plan for us from the beginning, "that we should be holy and blameless before Him." (Eph 1:4)

> For he has made known to us in all wisdom and insight the mystery of his will, according to his purpose which he set forth in Christ as a plan for the fulness of time, to unite all things in him, things in heaven and things on earth.[101]

The holiness of God is in a sense unapproachable, cloaked within the eternal and the infinite of the Godhead. Yet He has revealed something of Himself in history - in creation, in words entrusted to men, in gracious interventions into our darkness and struggle. God has created us with a destiny to more than we can comprehend: a vocation beyond our grasp or our imagination. But in the mysteries of supernatural faith and hope, we dare to look toward Him, and into the mystery of His holiness, with a humble "yes".

<u>The meaning of the name for us</u>

The meaning of the name for us is love. At every station in the interior liturgy, the meaning of the name is love. As we pray the *Our Father* along the path of our discipleship, our understanding of the name grows, as does our understanding of love. In the fullness of Christian life, beholding in the Son the face of the Father, we know love in simplicity and in perfection, because we behold Love: God is love.

The entire liturgy is a work of love, and a working of love: Christ, in love, is working love in us. In the understanding of St. Bernard, we see the developing and maturing of love in the three movements of His saving work. In this last movement, in the last station of this last movement, we see the fullness of this love flowing from the immediate worship of the Father in the Son. Here our charity finds its fullness: our charity is by grace a human participation in the divine charity of God. Our charity is but a tiny stream flowing from our tiny hearts, but merging into the rushing torrent of God's love, the love of the Father and the Son, the love of the divine breath, the Holy Spirit: here our love finds its origin, its meaning, its end.

What is the name of God? The name was revealed to Moses, to be guarded in the covenant that would prepare the way for the divine incarnation.

> Then Moses said to God, "If I come to the people of Israel and say to them, 'The God of your fathers has sent me to you,' and they ask me, 'What is his name?' What shall I say to them?" God said to Moses, "I AM WHO I AM." And he said, "Say this to the people of Israel, 'I AM has sent me to you.'"[102]

The mystery of this name draws us: it attracts us as it attracted Moses. We know that there is here a question we cannot contain in words, yet its answer we must find. Moses said, "I will turn aside and see this great sight, why the bush is not burnt." (Gen 3:3) The mystery can be approached only in the reverence shown by Moses as he approached the burning bush: in obedience he took off his shoes, because he was walking on holy ground. In this bush, burning yet not consumed, Moses saw the sign of the holy name: a love burning yet not consuming, a love flaming and radiating light and heat, yet not destroying. God is Absolute Being: God IS; God is personal, who must declare His Being as a subject: I AM WHO I AM. God in His Being is no static or dead thing: He is personal, and He is revealed in the sign of a bush burning yet not consumed.

The sign of the burning bush was revealed in the Church more personally, more intimately, in the sign of the Sacred

Heart of Jesus: His heart, aflame in an eternal burning love, unconsumed forever.

> Jesus knew and loved us each and all during his life, his agony and his Passion, and gave himself up for each one of us: "The Son of God. . . loved me and gave himself for me." He has loved us all with a human heart. For this reason, the Sacred Heart of Jesus, pierced by our sins and for our salvation,[Cf. Jn 19:34] "is quite rightly considered the chief sign and symbol of that. . . love with which the divine Redeemer continually loves the eternal Father and all human beings" without exception.[103]

The holy name is love: a burning love enflamed in the heart of the incarnate Son, revealing that roaring furnace of love that is the divine communion. Jesus has revealed the name to us: as we see Him, we see God.

The bush was not consumed. This is the love of this station of the interior liturgy: this is the perfection of love in a human person, a participation in the Sacred Heart of Jesus. This is the love of a saint, of a martyr who has not the fear of death - only the fear of failing to love. How can we fear the destruction of the body? The resurrection has exposed this lie of the evil one. How can we fear the loss of our friends, our career, our station in life? We see them through anointed eyes, as the loving eyes of Christ. How can we fear for our reputation, our seat in the synagogue, our place among the saints? God is our judge, and He is true. God's love is our great treasure: it does not consume, it does not destroy.

In the bosom of His name is our home. In His name the divine image finds its home and its meaning. Here, the human person finds humanity. The Vatican Council II saw into the nature of the human person most clearly :

> ... the Lord Jesus, when He prayed to the Father, "that all may be one. . . as we are one" (John 17:21-22) opened up vistas closed to human reason, for He implied a certain likeness between the union of the divine Persons, and the unity of

God's sons in truth and charity. This likeness reveals that man, who is the only creature on earth which God willed for itself, cannot fully find himself except through a sincere gift of himself.[104]

In the divine name we find ourselves: loved, loving; gifted, giving; self-emptying in joy, fulfilled; sharing with the Son in a complete "yes" for the Other, forever burning yet not consumed: finally, persons willed by God for ourselves. Christ has gone to prepare a place for us, that where He is, we may be. Here, beholding the face of the Father, is the divine communion of Sabbath rest. Here the work of the liturgy meets the rest of the Sabbath, and we are at peace.

Matrimony - the Sacrament of the Seventh Station

The sacrament that specifically illuminates this station, revealing its meaning and place in the holy liturgy, is the sacrament of Matrimony. This is the station of covenant, of the spiritual marriage of the soul with the divine Spouse. Here the inner meaning of covenant indeed is revealed: the meaning of covenant is love. This was the meaning in the beginning, in the first covenant given to man in the Garden. (Gen 2) This is the meaning of the first covenant graced in the new creation with the real presence of Christ, in the wedding at Cana. (Jn 2)

The mystery at the sacred center of marriage is the very mystery at the center of all mysteries: it is the mystery of love, of communion of persons. In the realm of the divine, the Holy Trinity is the central mystery of the faith: the mystery of divine communion, of three Persons yet one God. In the realm of humanity, in this most common yet sacred sacrament, we find this mysterious center to which is ordered all human community, all human culture and society: covenant in love, marriage. In marriage the two become one, and so present God to one another and to the world - a sign of the communion of divine Persons in Holy Trinity. Marriage also, in the mystery of two becoming one, presents that unity of persons that is the communion of Christ and His Church. (Eph 5:32)

True communion, in divine charity, is fruitful. Because of the essential fecundity in God who is charity, in God who is communion in the Holy Trinity, we may dare to say that charity is fruitful. Love, that is, charity, is essentially fruitful and by its nature it must necessarily be so. Whether human conjugal love brings forth the beautiful fruit of children, or whether the couple is by outward appearances barren: real love is fruitful. Whether the consecrated celibate in the Church, devoted in love to apostolic good works, sees the outward fruit of his labors or not: divine love is fruitful. Whether the contemplative recluse, confined to her cell in prayer and solitude for all her fertile years, ever sees the fruit flowing from her sacrifices and interior labors, still divine charity is fruitful.

Though the fig tree do not blossom,
> nor fruit be on the vines,

the produce of the olive fail
> and the fields yield no food,

the flock be cut off from the fold
> and there be no herd in the stalls,

yet I will rejoice in the LORD,
> I will joy in the God of my salvation.

GOD, the Lord, is my strength;
> he makes my feet like hinds' feet,

> he makes me tread upon my high places.[105]

Divine love, expressing itself in being ever _for_ the other, is always fruitful. This most fundamental mystery identified simultaneously with human love, with marriage, with communion, with consecrated celibacy, with God in His inner life the Holy Trinity, is illuminated for us in the world through this defining light of the Lord Jesus Christ: He is always *for* the other.

Jesus always did what was pleasing to the Father, ever obedient to His will. He said, "I have come down from heaven, not to do my own will, but the will of him who sent me." (Jn 6:38) He confessed His complete submission to the Father: "I can do nothing on my own authority; ... I seek not my own will but the will of him who sent me." (Jn 5:30) He confessed only a mysterious dependency and poverty in Himself, saying, "My teaching is not mine, but his who sent me." (Jn 7:16) Indeed, the Father "has given all things into his hand." (Jn 3:35) It was very important to the mission of Jesus that He reveal this truth! Jesus praised the Father that His disciples had learned, and "Now they know that everything that thou hast given me is from thee." (Jn 17:7)

This mysterious poverty in God, revealed to us in Christ Jesus, is also somehow His unfathomable wealth. All that He has is from the Father, and yet He can say, "All that the Father has is mine." (Jn 16:15) More than all that He has – even His very being, all that the Son is, is from the Father! We confess that the Son is "eternally begotten from the Father."[106] This profound phrase reveals the dynamic outpouring of life and love eternally proceeding in the infinite interior essence of God the Holy Trinity. We recite this phrase in the Mass, in the Nicene Creed, confessing again and again the crucial and central mystery of Trinity, of communion of Persons, of Three in One.

> ... eternally begotten of the Father, God from God, Light from Light, true God from true God, begotten, not made, of one Being with the Father. Through him all things were made. For us men and for our salvation, he came down from heaven: by the power of the Holy Spirit he was born of the Virgin Mary, and became man. For our sake he was crucified under Pontius Pilate; he suffered died and was buried. ....[107]

Together with being wholly of the Father, and for Him, we confess also that Jesus is wholly for us: "For us men and for our salvation, he came down from heaven .... For our sake He was crucified...." And His ministry for others did not deplete Him - He did not suffer loss, in the whole-hearted outpouring of Self in love for others! Exactly the opposite is revealed to us, that this outpouring of Self in humble love is rather nourishment for Him! Jesus could say, "My food is to do the will of him who sent me, and to accomplish his work." (Jn 4:34) This great and joyful mystery of His life is revealed to His saints in our own self-donation: the giving of ourselves is not death for us - it is life. To lose oneself for Christ is only to gain, and to find one's true vocation and meaning.

The dignity of marriage, of conjugal love, is not recognized by so many in our confused culture! Conjugal, sexual love is a great sign of the most defining mark of our nature - that we are made in the divine image. The two become one in love, fully, personally and most intimately. Conjugal love is expressed physically through the bodies of the two, and yet the experience of the union transcends the physical to embrace the full humanity of the man and the woman. It is the fullness of the persons in mutual self-gift that is expressed in conjugal love. In the sexual act, the man in his uniquely masculine way, and the woman in her uniquely feminine way, give themselves to the other and at the same time, receive the gift of the other. In this act, the deepest mystery of our nature is at least in part unveiled.

In this most beautiful and most mysterious action of conjugal, sexual love, which is of human kenosis, we peer into the inner life of God Himself. This is the infinite mystery of God in the dynamo of His inner being. Here again we find the mystery of the burning bush, the epiphany of the name of God, I AM WHO I AM, His very Being. The burning heart of God gives, and is never depleted! God is Love, God is Gift! This is the eternal and infinite kenosis of God: God gives and receives, overflows and outpours Himself infinitely, divinely, in the interiority of His nature. God is Trinity by nature, by nature the Father eternally begetting the Son, the Son eternally begotten by the Father, the Holy Spirit eternally spirating or processing from the Father and the Son: eternal Love, eternal Gift of God to God.

Kenosis, the whole gift of self, is necessary to us as men and women because we are made in His image. God loves, eternally being for the Other within the Holy Trinity. God made us this way, to be like Him. To be happy, we must love: we must become for the other. This is the grace of Matrimony: the grace to be for another, the grace of covenant love. The Church recognized this crucial, essential aspect of our human nature in the quote above, affirming that man "is the only creature on earth which God willed for itself," and yet he "cannot fully find himself except through a sincere gift of himself."[108]

Here the great dignity of the human person is revealed, grounded as it is in the divine image. Because we are, we are beloved by God and therefore worthy of dignity, or respect, and of the love of our brothers and sisters. And because we are persons made in His image, we are made to love and to be loved, to give and to receive, to be for the other and to find ourselves in self donation.

"God created man and woman together and willed each for the other."[109] In Matrimony, man and woman are graced to enter that covenant of mutual self-gift that expresses our vocation to the divine image, to being "for" the other. The nuptial mystery of life and being, first expressed through Adam and Eve and reaffirmed throughout human cultures and history, points us to our ultimate vocation to communion with God in the Holy Trinity, in the holiness of the most holy name. In this mystery the whole Christian life is summed: the whole of the sacraments, the whole of the liturgy, the whole of the interior life of prayer and communion:

> The entire Christian life bears the mark of the spousal love of Christ and the Church. Already Baptism, the entry into the People of God, is a nuptial mystery; it is so to speak the nuptial bath (Cf. Eph 5:26-27) which precedes the wedding feast, the Eucharist. Christian marriage in its turn becomes an efficacious sign, the sacrament of the covenant of Christ and the Church.[110]

The Virgin Mary and the station of the name

We have been commanded, from the beginning, to bear fruit. Fruit is the joy of our own hearts, and it is the joy of God who commands it of us. In the Garden we were told, "Be fruitful, and multiply, and fill the earth and subdue it...." (Gen 1:28) Jesus again commands fruitfulness, showing the deeper and spiritual meaning within it, saying, "By this my Father is glorified, that you bear much fruit, and so prove to be my disciples." (Jn 15:8) In the holy name of God is the origin of all our fruitfulness: in God the Holy Trinity, in the eternal generation of divine Persons within the fecundity of God who is love.

We are commanded into a human participation in the divine fruitfulness of God: we are created in His image, we are reborn in His name. In Mary we see the greatest human participation in the divine eternal generation in love! In Mary, through the "yes" of her loving obedience of faith, through this wholehearted self-gift to God, God answered with His own Self-Gift. God the Holy Spirit came to Mary, and enabled a new motherhood upon the earth. God the Holy Spirit "overshadowed" her, and from Mary came the Christ, the Son of God. Now her motherhood continues in us, the Church His mystical body: "We believe that the Holy Mother of God, the new Eve, Mother of the Church, continues in heaven to exercise her maternal role on behalf of the members of Christ"[111]

Here, in the summit of the interior liturgy, we find Mary. She waits in every station for her children, waiting upon them and loving them - but here, we come to know her most fully for who she is. Here, in the station that calls forth the grace of mystical marriage, we find the abundant fertility of her complete virginity. Here, in contemplative silence within the most holy inner sanctuary of the name, we hear the sound of human love complete in her simple "yes". This is the perfection of charity, the fulfillment of the interior liturgy, the intimate embrace of beatific truth.

Examination of Conscience in the Seventh Station

Can I ever cease contemplating the beauty of God in Mary? Can I pull away from her long enough, to serve her needs? They have no wine, she says, and the wedding is delayed - all wait, all become quiet, all watch the hand of the master. Do whatever He tells you, she says. Is the water prepared? Are all the containers full, to the brim? Is it all just as He ordered? Are we all ready?

Am I as thirsty as He is; am I as eager as He is, for the great wedding feast to proceed? Where do I waste His gifts? Where do I look away, distracted? How do I turn from the furrow, and neglect the straight path before me? When do I fail to see Him in her, and her in us all?

Prayer:

O Jesus,
through the Immaculate Heart of Mary,
I offer you my prayers, works,
joys, and sufferings of this day
in union with the Holy sacrifice of the Mass
throughout the world.
I offer them for the intentions

of your Sacred Heart:
the salvation of souls, reparation for sin,
the reunion of all Christians.
I offer them as I offer myself,
in union with Mary and all the saints,
with all your holy Church,
in the unity of the Holy Spirit.
Amen.[112]

The Spiritual Life	The First Stage			The Second Stage		The Third Stage	
Formation of the Apostles	Formation by following Jesus in His earthy ministry; up to the cross			Formation by the Resurrected Christ		Formation after Ascension: the abiding Holy Spirit	
Traditional Spirituality	The Purgative Stage; the Stage of the Beginners			The Illuminative Stage, the Stage of the Proficients		The Unitive Stage, the Stage of the Perfect	
St. Teresa's Interior Castle	The 1st Mansions	The 2nd Mansions	The 3rd Mansions	The 4th Mansions	The 5th Mansions	The 6th Mansions	The 7th Mansions
Holy Mass	The Liturgy of the Word			Consecration at the Altar		The Holy Communion	
Movements of the Interior Liturgy	The Interior Liturgy of the Word			The Consecration at the Altar of the Heart		Communion with Christ	
Stations of the Interior Liturgy	1st Station: Deliverance from Evil	2nd Station: Trial in Temptation	3rd Station: Mercy	4th Station: Consecration at the Altar	5th Station: Consecration in Suffering	6th Station: Ecclesial Communion	7th Station: Personal Communion
Petitions of the Our Father	Deliver us from evil.	Lead us not into temptation	Forgive us... as we forgive...	Give us this day our daily bread.	Thy will be done... as it is in heaven.	Thy kingdom come.	Hallowed be thy name.

Figure 3: Several perspectives on the spiritual life, correlated. This table - this book - should not be seen as "compartmentalizing" the spiritual life, nor as depersonalizing what is a most personal work of Christ in each human soul. Rather, we see here the normative pattern of Christ's work. His work begins and progresses toward the goal. Our part may be to resist Him and delay His work, or to cooperate and hasten it. Our path may be straight and true, or one of much wandering and many detours.

Conclusion and Summary

The *Our Father* is supremely the sacramental, liturgical prayer. It is the prayer of the entire saving work of Christ in the soul, His interior liturgy. Figure 3, on page 216, summarizes many of the correlations noted in this book concerning the *Our Father*, and the interior liturgy of Christ in the soul.

The *Our Father* is a unique gift from God, describing as it does the way that God wants us to pray. Without His direction we would hardly know up from down; without His prompting our prayer would remain in groans and sighs within us, too deep for words. (Rom 8:26) Yet He does teach us how to pray; He does show us the way of return to Him.

The *Our Father* prompts us to pray with the right words, in the right sequence – not because God needs these words or this sequence, but because we do. By means of grace descending, down through seven stations in an interior work in the soul, a human person is invited to ascend with Him and to Him. By means of grace given in portions as needed, as can be received, a human person is called to respond in steps, through seven stations. By means of grace cascading station by station through the interior liturgy down to where we are, the way of return is illuminated for us – and the work of return can proceed.

Christ, in the work of His sacred humanity, is the sacrament of our salvation. In the prayer the *Our Father*, we are led through a certain interior expression of Christ in His seven sacraments. Just as the seven sacraments of the Church are seven particular encounters with Christ in His saving work, so in the seven stations of the interior liturgy we encounter seven graces corresponding to His sacraments. The first movement of the saving work within is the Liturgy of the Word. This corresponds to the purgative stage of the beginners, of those first entering the interior life and discipleship. Within this movement are the first three stations of the interior liturgy, which correspond to the first three interior mansions in St. Teresa's *Interior Castle*.

1. The first station is the station of deliverance, of repentance and conversion to Christ. Here, empowered through our baptismal graces in Christ, we pray, "deliver us from evil."

2. The second station is the station of temptations, of trial and discernment of the heart. Here, strengthened by the graces of confirmation in Christ, we pray, "lead us not into temptation."

3. The third station is the station of confession, of reconciliation and mercy. Here, receiving the grace of confession to Christ, we pray, "forgive us our trespasses as we forgive those who trespass against us."

This third petition, importantly, is conditional. The conditional "as", linking the mercy we need from God for ourselves, with our need to be a source of mercy toward others, forms a bridge in our prayer to a dark night – the dark night of the senses. Here, our hearts are prepared to meet the Lord at the altar, the cross.

The second movement of the saving work within is the Liturgy of the Consecration at the Altar. This corresponds to the illuminative stage of the proficients, of those continuing in the interior life and discipleship. This great saving work emerges only through a first dark night, the night of the senses. Within this movement are the next two stations of the interior liturgy, which correspond to the next two interior mansions in St. Teresa's *Interior Castle*.

4. The fourth station is the station of our consecration at the altar of the cross of Christ. Here, we pray for the enabling

bread from heaven, our sustenance in Christ, the Holy Eucharist. We pray, "Give us this day our daily bread."

5. The fifth station is the station of anointing by Christ in our suffering. It is the station of His glory on the cross, and in some small measure, ours also. Through His embrace of the Father's will, even to His cross, our cross is thus illuminated and, in His grace, embraced. Here we pray, "Thy will be done on earth as it is in heaven."

This fifth petition, as was the third, is conditional. The conditional "as" here, linking our consecration to His will done on earth, with our loving gaze toward His will in heaven, forms another bridge in our prayer to a second dark night - the dark night of the spirit. Here, our souls are prepared to embrace the Lord in most intimate communion.

The third movement of the saving work within is the Liturgy of the Holy Communion. This corresponds to the unitive stage of the perfect, of those attaining the summit of the interior life and discipleship. This final movement of His liturgy emerges only through a second deep trial of darkness, the night of the spirit. Within this movement are the final two stations of the interior liturgy, which correspond to the final two interior mansions in St. Teresa's *Interior Castle*.

6. The sixth station is the station of service in holy mother the Church, the station of self-offering in her mission in Christ. Here, receiving a heart-priesthood in Christ, we pray, "Thy kingdom come."

7. The seventh station is the station of holy marriage with Christ, the station of union in the holy name. Here, made one by covenant we pray, "Hallowed be thy name."

The seventh station is also the final station, the station of waiting. We rest in Him there, and we await His coming for us, that we might be with Him where He is. He is ever before the Father, in the communion of infinite love, and there He awaits us. In the final work of our return, we will enter this communion most completely, saying in the words of the Son and in Him, and through the Holy Spirit, "Our Father, who art in heaven!"

The *Our Father* is also the supreme pastoral prayer, the prayer in Christ for the people of God. After this meditation on the prayer, we are able to enter more whole-heartedly into communion with Jesus, the Good Shepherd, in His prayer for us all. As we ponder the stations of the interior liturgy and the special graces, challenges and opportunities of each station, we see how we are called to a particular pastoral awareness of every brother and sister in his and her own interior liturgy.

> See that you do not despise one of these little ones; for I tell you that in heaven their angels always behold the face of my Father who is in heaven. What do you think? If a man has a hundred sheep, and one of them has gone astray, does he not leave the ninety-nine on the mountains and go in search of the one that went astray? And if he finds it, truly, I say to you, he rejoices over it more than over the ninety-nine that never went astray. So it is not the will of my Father who is in heaven that one of these little ones should perish.[113]

The Church is diverse in many ways - her gifts and her graces are distributed among the members in the wisdom of the Spirit. She is diverse also in the sense that her members are spread out through all the stations of the interior liturgy, through all the stages of the great in-gathering of the Lord. As pilgrims, some are at the very beginning of the journey, barely free from the dark clutches of sin and death. Some others are lights for the whole Church, models of holiness, at the very threshold of the Beatific Vision. Others in the journey are dispersed from the first station to the last, filling every stage of the interior life, in every movement of the liturgy.

As we pray the *Our Father*, we are invited time and time again, petition by petition, to enter the saving work of the Lord with full, active and conscious participation. We are called into His liturgy, as He unfolds the work within us. In the beginning we can only receive, like the spiritual children that we are, the nurturing milk of the saving Word: "Like newborn babes, long for the pure spiritual milk, that by it you may grow up to salvation; for you have tasted the kindness of the Lord." (1 Pet 2:2-3) We must guard and nurture the great graces given us. We can hardly be conscious of the many souls struggling around us - the many who are in truth our brothers and sisters! Like a drowning man just thrown a life preserver, we can do little more than grasp the saving help and hold fast.

As the liturgy progresses in us, if our ears and hearts are open, we begin to hear - and hearing, we begin to see. St. Peter exhorts us to listen, to treasure the sacred apostolic witness of truth: "And we have the prophetic word made more sure. You will do well to pay attention to this as to a lamp shining in a dark place, until the day dawns and the morning star rises in your hearts." (2 Pet 1:19) Thus we pray, and stay close to the Word and the precious grace in Holy Scripture. This first work of Christ in us, His Liturgy of the Word, is the essential foundation: allow it to be secure, firmly planted, true!

It may be that pastoral awareness is begun in the soul even in this first work. It is, however, in the second great movement of His intervention in the soul, the interior liturgy of consecration at the altar of the heart, when this awareness of our brothers and our sisters is made more clear. In this liturgy of consecration we stand at the foot of the cross; we hear our Lord Jesus give "the disciple whom he loved" to his mother: "Woman, behold your son." Here heart-consecration is made possible by the power of the Word of God: consecration to mother Church, consecration to Jesus through Mary. Here also individualism at the expense of personhood can end, by the power of the Word of God. In the communion of the saints gathered under Mary, we find solidarity with all humankind regained, after its loss under Eve. In Mary the human family is restored: "Behold, your mother." (Jn 19:26-27)

Here the pastoral dimension of this great prayer is revealed, in the glorious light of outpoured love from the cross. This prayer calls us to heart-felt communion with all men as we pray "Our Father." Whom can we omit? We can omit none! This prayer "excludes no one."[114] God so loved all human persons, each formed in His divine image, that He sent His son to save us and gather us into His love. (Jn 3:16) Beginning in the liturgy of consecration, we are invited and empowered to present ourselves with Him in the great self-donation that is love. Here, with Him and in Him, we become in some way shepherds too - shepherds with Peter, and mothers with Mary.

Beginning in earnest in the second great movement, but reaching a fullness in the third - the liturgy of communion - we enter the joy of our Master, the joy of self-gift. Here, the *Our Father* is prayed in the roaring furnace of the Sacred Heart, sung amid a chorus of myriads and thousands, angels and saints and the beloved of the Lord all together in a solidarity of love and obedience and worship, in prayer for all the human family. Here, in full and active and conscious participation in the saving work of God, we cast out our net of prayer to all the stations of the liturgy and beyond. We exclude no one; we reach out to all with the saving love of Christ.

We long for a holy witness to Christ, for the unity of the faith, that all may know that the Father sent Jesus and that Jesus sent us. So we pray first for the Church, that through the Church the saving Gospel might be preached to all the world. Our prayer reaches from the Sacred Heart out to embrace all who look to Him. We pray in the intimacy of this Heart, "hallowed be thy name!" We pray for those offering themselves in union with Him in ministry, "thy kingdom come!" We pray for those nourished in the bread of heaven, opening their own hearts to the saving obedience of Christ: "thy will be done on earth as it is in heaven." We pray for those standing at the altar of consecration, hungry for that sacred power, that eternal bread, that divine presence: "give us this day our daily bread." We pray for those near to the altar, daring to open their hearts to the mercy of God, daring in His grace to trust in darkness: "forgive us our trespasses as we forgive those who trespass against us." We pray for those young souls who have overcome in the battle against sin and who now face the interior war of temptations: "lead us not into temptation." We pray, finally, for those just escaped from the clutches of the evil one and his lies, for those who have now begun the greatest engagement of all humanity - our vocation into Christ and His holiness: "deliver us from evil." Amen.

Addendum - Vocabulary

The <u>anaphora</u>, the Eucharistic Prayer: this is the liturgical prayer of thanksgiving and consecration, the center of the celebration. This includes specifically thanksgiving, acclamation in the sanctus, the epiclesis, the institutional narrative and consecration, the anamnesis or remembrance, the offering and the intercessions, and the final doxology.

The <u>epiclesis</u> ("invocation upon") is the prayer within the anaphora, in which the priest begs the Father to send the Holy Spirit who sanctifies, that the gifts offered may become the body and blood of Christ - and also, that the faithful who receive Holy Eucharist may themselves become a living offering to God. (see Rom 12:1) The epiclesis is a prayer of our deep need and dependence, and of our openness to the necessary work of God. "The Church therefore asks the Father to send the Holy Spirit to make the lives of the faithful a living sacrifice to God by their spiritual transformation into the image of Christ, by concern for the Church's unity, and by taking part in her mission through the witness and service of charity." (Catechism 1109)

<u>Kenosis</u> - This noun is derived from the verb in Phil 2:7, "he emptied himself." I have found no better sense of meaning and significance of this crucial word, that that given by Jean Corbon:
"The Son remains God when he becomes incarnate but he divests himself of his glory to the point of being 'unrecognizable' (see Is 53:2-3). Kenosis is the properly divine way of loving: becoming a human being without reservation and without calling for recognition or compelling it. Kenosis refers first to the self-emptying of the Word in the incarnation but this is completed in the self-emptying of the Spirit in the Church, while it also reveals the self-emptying of the living God in creation. The mystery of the covenant stands under the sign of kenosis, for the more far-reaching the covenant, the more complete the union. Our divinization comes through the meeting of the kenosis of God with the kenosis of the human being; the fundamental requirement of the Gospel can therefore be stated as follows: we shall be one with Christ to the extent that we 'lose' ourselves for him."[115]

End Notes

1   R. Thomas Richard, *The Ordinary Path to Holiness* (New York, The Society of St. Paul, Alba House, 2003).

2   Love here meaning the theological virtue of charity: love for God because of Who He is, and love for others because of God and in God.

3   Eph 2:8-9

4   Gen 1:27-28

5   *The Catechism of the Catholic Church*, 2427

6   *Catechism* 1074, SC 10

7   *Catechism* 1324, LG 11

8   *Catechism* 1324, PO 5

9   Vatican II Documents, SC 14

10   *Catechism* 1124

11   *Catechism* 1073

12   Lk 10: 25-28

13   see, for example, St. Bernard's degrees of love in *The Ordinary Path to Holiness*, 25-28.

14   *Catechism* 260

15   *Catechism* 1373

16   *Catechism* 1413

17   *Catechism* 1324, LG 11

18   Lk 10:38-42

19   St. John Vianney, His *Catechetical Instructions*, Ch. 8: On Prayer

20   *Catechism* 2564

21   *Catechism* 2564

22   Rom 8:26

23   Thomas Aquinas, *Summa Theologica* I, Q37, art. 1

24   Thomas Aquinas, *S.T.* I, Q38, art. 2

25   Thomas Aquinas, *S.T.* II-II,Q.83,art.9

26   Mt 5-7

27   *Catechism* 467, cf. Heb 4:15

28   Thomas Aquinas, *S.T.* II-II,Q.83,art.9

29   *Catechism* 2652

30   *The Ordinary Path to Holiness*, ch. 5, p. 131-150

31   *Catechism* 1141, SC 14

32   *Catechism* 774
33   *Catechism* 1213
34   *Catechism* 1285
35   *Catechism* 1521
36   Section Title preceding *Catechism* 1533
37   *Catechism* 1534
38   *Catechism* 1548
39   *Catechism* 234
40   *Catechism* 2815
41   *Catechism* 2777, 2783, 2793
42   *The Ordinary Path to Holiness*, 88-109
43   *The Ordinary Path to Holiness*, 109, 138
44   Mt 11:28-30
45   Mt 19:16-24
46   Mt 5:29-30
47   Lk 5:36-39
48   Mt 19:27
49   Mk 12: 29-34
50   Heb 2:14-15
51   *Catechism* 1213
52   *Catechism* 1861
53   see, for example, *The Ordinary Path to Holiness*, ch. 4, 83-130
54   Prov 2:1-5
55   *The Ordinary Path to Holiness*, 139
56   Mk 7:20-23
57   *Catechism* 1263
58   *Catechism* 1264
59   *Catechism* 2846
60   James 1:2-8
61   James 1:12-15
62   *Catechism* 2848
63   *Catechism* 1285
64   *Catechism* 1303
65   *The Ordinary Path to Holiness*, 92-96
66   *The Ordinary Path to Holiness*, 99
67   *Catechism* 133
68   *The Ordinary Path to Holiness*, 140
69   Mt 18:23-35
70   *Catechism* 2840

71   *Catechism* 1822
72   *Catechism* 1826-29
73   Ps 77:1-13
74   *The Ordinary Path to Holiness*, 88-89
75   *The Ordinary Path to Holiness*, 108
76   *Catechism* 1352-3
77   *Catechism* 1324
78   *Catechism* 969
79   *Catechism* 1381: St. Thomas Aquinas (attr.), Adoro te devote; tr. Gerard Manley Hopkins
80   *The Ordinary Path to Holiness*, 109
81   Rom 12:1-2
82   *Catechism* 1520
83   *Catechism* 1521
84   *Three Ages* vol. 2 p. 358
85   *The Ordinary Path to Holiness*, 94 ff.
86   *Catechism* 506, LG 63; cf. 1 Cor 7:34-35
87   *Gaudium et Spes* 24
88   *Catechism* 2617
89   *Catechism* 264
90   St. John Vianney, *Catechism on Prayer*
91   *The Ordinary Path to Holiness*, 110
92   Mt 28: 19-20
93   Eph 4:11-13
94   *Catechism* 972
95   *Catechism* 1547
96   *St. Francis of Assisi*, Omer Englebert, Servant Books, Ann Arbor 1979, p. 171-2
97   *The Ordinary Path to Holiness*, 111
98   *Catechism* 234
99   *Catechism* 2815
100 *Catechism* 2809, Cf. Ps 8; Is 6:3
101 Eph 1: 9-10
102 Ex. 3:13-14
103 *Catechism* 478
104 *Gaudium et Spes* 24
105 Hab 3:17-19
106 *Catechism* 2789
107 From The Nicene Creed
108 *Gaudium et Spes* 24

109 *Catechism* 371

110 *Catechism* 1617

111 *Catechism* 975

112 From a traditional Catholic prayer of morning offering

113 Mt 18:10-14

114 *Catechism* 2792

115 Jean Corbon, *The Wellspring of Worship* trans. Matthew O'Connell. (New York: Paulist Press, 1988), 6-7